Way

WAYS OF LIFE

Connie Mckenzie

Published in 2020
with the help of Lumphanan Press
9 Anderson Terrace, Tarland
Aberdeenshire, AB34 4YH

www.lumphananpress.co.uk

Front cover: Marischal College, Aberdeen

Back cover: engraving of Winchester Cathedral by J Hawksworth,
after a sketch by George Shepheard

ISBN: 978-1-5272-8100-4

Printed and bound by Imprint Digital,
Upton Pyne, Devon, UK

One

Two coaches were parked on the road by the side of the church. A shiny black limousine had just drawn up on at the pavement in front of a flight of wide granite steps, leading to the entrance of this elegant building with its clock tower. A second limousine was making progress towards the church, bearing myself and my father. Along the pavements, small groups of people unable to attend the service in church, waved in honour of the local bride. It came as a surprise to me, that I felt so foolish; was it really necessary to dress a girl up in a long white dress, carrying a bouquet of flowers, just to be married? Perhaps, my long engagement brought me a degree of cynicism. This was tradition, and here I was, with my mother's exquisitely embroidered veil covering my face, and holding a bouquet of huge Arum lilies, my favourite flowers.

My bridesmaids were my sisters, Flora, now grown up, and Christine, just nine, along with Norma, Sydney's niece of the same age. They were in place, waiting to attach my long train to the hooks at its sides, and follow me up the sparkling steps. Soon, I was on the arm of my father. There was movement from within, as the organ played an introit and my father just had time to whisper "when you come out, you'll still be my girl" The organ burst into music for our walk towards the altar. I turned to look up and smile to my friends in the choir, where I usually sat and sang. The church was full of smiling faces. My soon-to-be husband looked round in greeting, as I approached his side, saying "you look beautiful "Thank you", I said in reply, wondering who had promoted such a remark, so out of character, even if he thought it!

The ceremony over, we emerged into a cool, but bright day. The Brahn See, a mystic of the McKenzie clan, had forecast that when Britain had three queens, winter would become summer and summer winter. This forecast was much the case in 1954, when Queen Mary was still alive, Queen Elizabeth, the Queen Mother, and our present Queen Elizabeth on the throne. Greetings over, and good wishes expressed by those not attending the reception in Aberdeen, the hired cars moved off for The Royal Hotel, followed by the coaches parked on the side road.

My family stood in the entrance hall of the hotel to greet our guests, some of whom had come from as far as London and Blackpool. The usual introductions were made, and soon, a lively party was making its way to the ballroom where a long table stretched the length of the room with a table set at right angles for the wedding party and family members, Spring flowers decorated both tables. All drinks were to be at the expense of Mr Cruden Sen. to include all toasts, wine to accompany the meal, and those ordered throughout the afternoon and evening.

The lives of the bride and groom were graphically described, by the minister, family members, and neighbours. I did notice that The Reverend Grant's whisky glass had to be topped up twice before any toasts were proposed. My bridesmaids all knew how to dance the Eightsome reel and Duke of Perth. They look so lovely in their pale mauve dresses and floral headbands. My now brother-in-law, Bill, danced with my youngest sister, Marion, much to her delight. At the age of six, she had been precluded from most of the wedding preparations, but now felt very important. Although celebrations were to continue until ten thirty, our train left the station for Edinburgh at eight o'clock The age old question arose, how to leave a Scottish wedding unimpeded by guests. Bill came to the rescue. His dance partner was upstairs preparing for bed, so he was able to take our luggage the short distance to the station, and arrange for it to be put on board the train for Edinburgh. This still left the problem of our escape unnoticed. Here, Sydney had a stroke of luck. A neighbour attending the wedding, who owned a trawler, had come in that morning with an unusually large catch of fish, and was broadcasting its profits to the company. It was he who led the followers in our pursuit, throwing ten bob and pound notes behind him, much to the glee of those following and breaking off to collect the bounty. At the main concourse of the station Sydney and I were ahead as Mr Buchan flung more notes into the air, and we were able to watch as our guests bent to pick up the money.

Our companion to Edinburgh was a young Spaniard, and since Sydney had a dux medal from school for Spanish, the two conversed in Spanish without much input from me. I heard an invitation being issued, and thought I could learn enough of the language for us to accept. That would never happen. Sydney had no desire to visit "foreign parts" The hills and lochs of Scotland were enough for him.

The honeymoon in Edinburgh followed roughly the same pattern as that of my parents, some twenty five years before, but we did not stay at The Cockburn, lodging instead in a small hotel called 'Sutties" This was housing theatrical people at the time, including Syd James. It was interesting to see them out of character and hear their complaints about Edinburgh.

Of course the castle was visited, and we poked our noses into Mary King Close which had been closed up during a visit of the plague and was now opened up as it had been left. Shops still had merchandise from that time and hooks hung from the ceiling of the butcher's shop. Its far exit can be seen from Geddes Street, high above the pavement where it once emerged near to The Nor Loch before it was drained to become part of Princes Street Gardens.

The Botanic Gardens also attracted us with its well – planned areas of woodland and large, unusual plants. Replicas in stone of huge tortoises from The Galapagos Islands stood by the entrance. Much of our time was spent in The Museum of Antiquities where so may strange artifacts were on display. We were to seek out the Roman Camp near Culter and visit 'Standing Stones' with ancient script.

Upon our return to Aberdeen, it was obvious that nothing of importance and been missed during the week of our visit to Edinburgh. Before leaving, we had secured a lodging of sitting room and bedroom, with use of kitchen, bathroom and garden. This was part of a semi-detatched house in Cranford Road, some three miles from my family home in Cults. Our landlady, Mrs Wright, a tall, lean lady, had been brought up in a small Aberdeenshire village. She entered our rooms all the time we were out, which we resented after a time. Her poor husband, now retired, had been a commercial traveller, and was pleasant when encountered alone. He was not allowed opinions of his own, and had no friends. When his wife went to market to buy fish for their cat, he took delight in showing me the garden. A bigger treat came when my young sisters came to visit, and "Mrs" was out. He played cards with them, and listened to their tales. MacGregor, the cat was huge, disdainful, and wise. He knew when fish was to arrive, and positioned himself on the last rung of the staircase, so that he could follow his mistress into the kitchen on her return and make sure his food was being prepared. Quite often, if we returned late, MacGregor would be in our room, sitting amongst the ornaments in the display cabinet, his black body and white front going almost unnoticed. If the lid of the piano was open, he would step down on to the notes, searching for where the sound was coming.

Sydney was back at work, cycling the short distance to the office in Queens Gate. My job was now to find a house or flat which we could afford to buy. My search encompassed the whole city, mainly within a radius from the office of three miles. One exception was a house in Cults, near Fairview. Although I viewed over a hundred properties, I remained attracted to a new development on the outskirts of the city. This offered the latest technology of the time: granite-faced houses, not solid granite, as people were used to, fitted kitchens, and a machine for washing clothes. This was my dream, but for one snag, namely the feu duty. It was very high, and people said the houses were over-priced. Thus ended my search for a completely new house at Airy Hall. A house came on the market in the next street, Duthie Terrace. This house was solid granite, with pitch pine wood-work. Its feu duty was very low for its accommodation, but no improvements had been carried out since its erection in nineteen twelve. This proved to be quite a bonus, since the interior walls were white, covered in plastic-like, embossed paper. The white staircase curved attractively at the last step. There was no hint of the dark brown decoration which became popular after the first world war. A bathroom and toilet occupied the space at the turn of the staircase, above the "maid's room", Farther on, a wide corridor with windows gave access to three bedrooms. The large sitting room with its square bay window, sported an enormous white marble fireplace. Above, cornices adorned the ceiling and surrounding walls. This charm was lost on me. It was alright for the older generation, but not for me, in spite of congratulations from many people at finding such a gem. Towards the end of nineteen fifty four, we moved into this 'gem' for the amazing cost of one thousand, four hundred pounds. Seeing the predicament of us in a big, old-fashioned property, both families gave aid. My father attended to any electrical work, and soon had the garden in good shape for spring planting. Sydney's father arranged for someone to bring paint and decorate for us. Isaac Spencers paint was used, just like on the base of trawlers, so very hard-wearing. Sydney got into his swimming trunks, and with blow lamp stripped the bath down to its cast iron form to be painted in a substance which would 'last forever'.

The deposit of ten per cent of the buying price had seemed reasonable at the time and was less than my dowry. However, the Co-Operative Building Society had worries about our ability to repay the loan which we had sought. To start with, in those days, only the husband's salary was taken into account. I was asked did my husband drink, and pointed out that he neither drank on a regular basis, nor did he smoke. I had been asked to fill in a questionnaire about our lifestyle which had to be countersigned by my husband and one adult. Here my father -in -law stepped in, offering to be guarantor for the amount outstanding on the purchase. The monthly repayments were not forthcoming until we had occupied the property for over a week. This uncertainty did not rest well with us, it being difficult to assess what furnishings we could afford.

The front door opened onto a tiled vestibule and through another door into a wide corridor leading to the curved staircase and at its end a right hand turn into another large room, used as a dining room off which a door led into a small room described as the 'maid's room' The scullery comwash house faced the garden and was about twelve feet square, excluding the coalhouse by the back door. In the far corner sat the huge concrete wash boiler with steps to reach the hole in its top where water could be poured in for the boiling of laundry Below was a hole in the side for setting a fire to bring the water to boiling point. A touch of modernization came in the form of two wash skins alongside the original sink. The big problem for us was lack of money. Despite saving as much as possible, this property needed money far beyond our means. Again our families were able to step in with two needs, two arm chairs. Wedding presents were much appreciated, especially gifts of money.

There was a second-hand shop at The Castlegate in Aberdeen; Cocky Hunter's. My days were spent viewing its stock and scanning the local newspapers for where there would be sales or household auctions [roups]. Roups proved very productive. Old fashioned items, suitable for our home were selling for knock – down prices. Provost Meff's late house proved a helpful source of requirements. I bought two carpets, one mostly brown which I did not like, but of good quality for the dining rooms and a large poorer quality one, but of attractive colouring, for the drawing room. Added to the carpets, I was able to purchase a brass coal skuttle and a pair of fire irons. We had turned down the offer of a brown three piece suite from the family, instead buying an enormous sofa in a greenish colour, hidden under its brown loose cover; a real bargain.

By spring time, our home was quite presentable. My mother brought my sisters and some friends for tea at regular intervals. Sydney's family made intermittent visits mainly in the evenings. With little money, and the garden planted up, I began to feel the need for some activity other than entertaining the family and household duties. I broached the subject with Sydney and his solution was that I attend to everything pertaining to the household, all finances, all hiring of services, and that it is how it remained for nearly sixty years – women's lib, or just equal division of labour??

My next door neighbour was a farmer's widow from Deeside, rolling in wealth, but watchful of every penny, fearful of anyone finding out her financial status. In those days wills were published in the press, and commented on by all and sundry. It was a mark of disgrace if a substantial amount appeared in a newspaper and the deceased had been mean to the church and charities during their lifetime or in bequests at the end.

My kind and generous neighbour had a keen sense of humour, and I remember her brushing earth off potatoes which she was about purchase from our local 'tattie man' and remarking 'Its yer tatties I'm buying, nae yer ferm'. She was to prove her worth in many ways during our short stay in Duthie Terrace.

Christmas and New Year had come and gone with its steady stream of family visits and parties with friends. At each event I cooked a haunch of venison, ordered by Sydney from the office, and brought from Drummond Hill Forest. It was a welcome change from the poultry usually served up. The pudding had to be Clootie dumpling, more or less, a Christmas cake wrapped in muslin cloth and steamed for several hours. Its aroma and steam always raised a cheer from the waiting guests as brandy was poured over and set alight.

By the end of January, I was harbouring the thought that I might be pregnant. My neighbour more or less confirmed this by remarking that I might need a wider coat. Mother said nothing. Spring days were filled with gardening and garnering objects for the house. Sydney's brother visited from Blackpool, where he and his family occupied a large house and were affluent enough to purchase all their needs. Both he and his wife were full of suggestions about velvet curtains for the dining room and plans for the maid's room, all of which we had no prospect of affording.

Eventually I consulted my dear doctors in Cults about my pregnancy. The practice was shared between husband and wife, Dr Jean and Dr Charlie. They confirmed my hope that Sydney and I would be parents sometime in the summer. Charles asked had I told my mother yet and advised that I keep quiet for a bit 'you know the kind of fuss which will be made'

In late spring, Sydney and I made a visit to his brother's wooden chalet at Coille-a-Creach, by the river Dee. There, we were part of a line of holiday homes on what seemed to be common ground. We walked and climbed all the nearby paths and, of course took a bus to Braemar, walking more and visiting Jock and Jessie's cottage, now occupied in summer by a young couple from the village. Already the village seemed to have lost some of its previous sparkle. The grounds of Kindrochit were not quite as tidy, the productive garden had not been planted up. The garage complex had obviously not been in use for some time. Although the feeling was of partial neglect and minds focused mainly on The Gathering and day trippers, the hotels seemed busy for springtime. There was little evidence of looking towards a season when long-term visitors of great affluence would occupy the large granite lodges and be part of village life throughout the summer. It puzzled me somewhat to find it so.

Back in Aberdeen, I continued the habit of meeting Sydney somewhere in Forest Avenue on his way back from the office. By the end of June, it was more than obvious that a baby was expected. My old green jacket just about covered my bulging form, and could be thrown away when the waiting was over. Everything was ready, and a new black high pram was waiting to be delivered to be put in the bay window to act as a piece of furniture.

David arrived on the second of August, one month before the predicted date. He was delivered in Aberdeen Royal Infirmary, where it was expected that new mothers would remain in bed for at least a week after birth. My sister, Flora kindly took a week off her work in Dundee to look after the home while mother and baby were in hospital. Her main memory was of burning the mince on her first day in charge. Fortunately there was a branch of The Co-op at the top of Duthie Terrace, just yards away, and she was able to replace pan and contents without delay. Home-coming was the signal for a relay of visits from relatives. My two young sisters were agog, more with the high pram and whether they could reach the handle and move it around, than with the baby inside. It became quite an obsession, pushing the pram, and steps had to be counted so that neither could possess the task longer than the other.

It was with some pride, that I walked up Forest Avenue to meet Sydney on his way home. Colleagues went out of their way to see the new arrival and one man in particular doted on David.

He was middle-aged, living with his mother. One could wonder if his life was frustrated by the inability to have a wife and family of his own. In those days, it was illegal to form an intimate relationship with another man. Soon, I was requested to come to the office at closing time so that David could be admired and me congratulated and showered with gifts. Indeed, it was quite a family event.

Dr Charlie became a regular caller, bringing weighing machine and news of Cults. He did not advise me to attend the baby clinic, except for orange juice and cod liver oil; "the clinic is where you pick up any infection going. I will weigh David and make sure you are both doing well."

By November, Sydney's Aunt Annie had a heart condition and being a widow without children, had no one to help her recovery. None of her sisters was able to offer a temporary home, so it fell to Sydney and me to lend support. Aunt Annie had emigrated to Australia and on her decision to return to Aberdeen, had met a Dutchman on the sea journey and became Mrs Klemp. She did not want children, her life having centred round caring for nieces and nephews, in particular a girl named Violet, who was quite severely handicapped and with a heart condition which was terminal. It was thought that help would be needed for a couple of weeks at most, but her sojourn extended to two months.

This thin, sparse lady proved quite an asset to me. Although unable to move far she could just reach the bathroom to wash and return to bed with help. Her instinct to look after a child had not deserted her, and each day she requested that 'the babe' be brought to her bed. David loved this hour of attention, and I valued the opportunity to cook and clean without interruption.

Two of Aunty Annie's sisters did visit her. Helen was emaciated with pointed nose and chin, who found fault with the world. By contrast, Lizzie was a very large lady, tall and stout with foot problems which occupied most of her conversation. Both held the opinion that it was bad for Annie to have David visit her in bed, but the answer came in Aunt Annie's shake of her head. Both were gone by the time Sydney arrived home from the office. He was not anxious to meet either owing to a family feud regarding support for the two handicapped members of the family, namely cousin Violet, already mentioned, and Bert, Sydney's blind and physically-handicapped brother. Apparently, more help had been given to Violet that to Bert, which did not go down well with Sydney's mother, now dead for several years.

Aunt Annie was a good guest. She was Episcopalian, well read and well travelled. Our conversations ranged over religion, Aberdeen in the old days, and Australia, which she had to leave to come back to look after her failing mother, but which brought her in middle age, a tall, bouncy husband, who like Annie had a deep love of children, always putting his hand in his pocket for a half-crown to give to them.

Aunt Annie had been with us for over six weeks when pronounced fit enough to go home to her house in Allanvale, near to Allanvale Cemetery, where some years later, she would be laid to rest.

Two

My mother had not approved of my taking Sydney's aunt for such a long spell. She felt someone else could have stepped in for some of the time. The fact that I received a pair of flannelette sheets, as recompense for over six weeks' lodging was scoffed at. For my part, I had enjoyed her stay; my only dilemma being that my husband liked his food well sweetened, while Annie was not a sweet tooth, turning her nose up at my apple crumble.

David was baptised at this time. The ceremony took place in the drawing room at Duthie Terrace, so that his uncle Bert could attend in his wheelchair. Reverend Grant, my minister from Cults arrived to conduct the baptism and brought his wife. Years later I was sent a photograph of the minister celebrating his one hundred and fifth birthday.

Nineteen fifty six would soon be upon us. Days were grey and snow lay deep in the garden. Outings were short until the end of February when conditions became more spring-like. Roads were clear enough for me to visit Fairview with baby in pram, so that my sisters could push it around the garden.

Change was upon us. Sydney had been selected for promotion, and allocated to head office in Saville Row, London. Pleasure was mixed with panic – sell our house we had worked so hard to make comfortable, find new accommodation near the city – a task surely beyond our expertise. It was decided that the house could catch the spring market, and that David and I would stay at Fairview, so that he could get to know his aunts and grandparents before moving south. It was the best solution, although I grieved that Sydney was missing those early small steps in David's progress. Mr Gray, son of my father's solicitor, and now of Gray and Kellas, Aberdeen, handled the sale. The usual crop of disinterested viewers arrived over the next two weeks, pointing out all manner of defects.

Due to a sickness bug going around, I was in bed for two days when my mother came to look after me and divert any viewers to another date.

One caller on behalf of his daughter was a friend of my father and could not be fobbed off; he was brought in, tea was made and he allowed to roam the house at will, except for my room. His appraisal was encouraging, egged on by my mother, and Mr Gray had a firm offer. In Scotland that was binding if accepted. Two more offers were present, only marginally above the asking price. Where several viewers were interested; a mini auction could develop with a deadline when offers were to be opened and the new owner declared. Mr Gray arrived to tell us that an offer of two thousand, two hundred pounds had been accepted on Sydney's behalf and a date three weeks hence for the keys to be handed over.

Little time was left for regrets, although I was beginning to regard this home with much affection. Our hard work had paid off, the profit of eight hundred pounds seemed like a fortune to us – a profit of 60%. This being a government move, all expenditure would attract allowances. The removal and storage would be paid for along with Sydney's accommodation expenses in London. Packing was to be carried out by Shore Porters, an Aberdeen firm established in fourteen ninety two. I had washed, cleaned and ordered goods into sections for easy unloading. It was described by the removal men as 'a military operation', and each of my subsequent removals followed the same pattern.

Cults was a breath of fresh air, and the garden at Fairview was strikingly beautiful with its roses clinging to the granite walls, and vegetables planted in neat rows beyond a mass of annuals bordering the middle path. Outside, just yards away ran the River Dee, with The Shakkin' Brig making a crossing to the far side of the river. Alongside the path going uphill to the village, ran The Den Burn, gurgling its way to the river. It called to mind the time when The Dee had burst its banks, flooding our garden and reaching the step at the back door.

This was to be my home for six weeks, seeing David flourish in the company of my young sisters, and taking note of the grey horse in the farmer's field next door. Mr Douglas did little farming. His land was regularly flooded, for which he could claim compensation from the government. Mrs Douglas was Caribbean birth and president of some organisation. Both she and her husband were keen Scottish Dancers and could be seen crossing the white bridge on Saturday evenings bound for Ardoe Hall on the other side of the river where dancing took place. This was a mixed race family, although not recognised in such terms. It was never spoken about or even wondered about to my knowledge. One daughter was talented in dance, being included in the cast of The Nutcracker when it was performed in His Majesty's Theatre, Aberdeen. She went on to have a career in Ballet. Residents in Cults turned out to see their 'vegetable man's' daughter perform for them. At the bus stop they praised the freshness of his produce, little knowing that most of it was bought at knock-down price in The Green, the market in Aberdeen. It was remarked that he must be very proud of his daughter and asked what he was doing to mark her success. His reply came that he had bought himself a new set of dentures because his speech had become 'a bit untidy'.

The farm was quite dilapidated, doors tied with string and rats and mice running out from holes at the foot. There was an abundance of cats running around, but to little effect. On one visit made by my mother on church business, a cat jumped out of the kettle when the lid was removed. Cat was just shewed away and kettle filled for the customary cup of tea. Mother was not impressed. To supplement income on the farm, rooms were let to summer visitors. From our house, we could view these families trundle cases round the bend on the steep decline towards the farm. The attraction of Cults with its river and park must have been overwhelming for these unsuspecting holiday-makers. A few did stay, but a more usual sight was of those trundling back up the hill on their journey home. Almost no baking took place, everything being sourced from the bakery or brought from Aberdeen. Their landlady had her head in a book; books were an addiction for her, and she was well informed.

My stay at Fairview gave me the opportunity to retrace old walks by the river and renew old friendships with shopkeepers and others in the village. I was invited to re-join the choir for the short time I had and was able to walk home from church with Bertie Grant, my old teacher of Latin. Two spinsters, Miss Skakles sang in the choir and lived nearby. Bunty was small and round with a penchant for hat pins, having at least three in any one hat. When asked the reason for the pins by one of my sisters, her reply was 'would anyone be bold enough to accost me at night?'. Her sister was gaunt and slim. They had a nephew living with them who was a minister of a church just north of Aberdeen.

Mr Cordiner stopped his car upon recognising me from the office at Queen's Gate. He was a large timber merchant who visited the office on many occasions. Billy Graham, the American evangelist, was his guest during his stay in Aberdeen. David was not neglected during this time, there was always a babysitter on hand in home or garden.

Sydney's family visited from time to time, getting to know my parents and sisters. Father Cruden had been widowed before the outbreak of war and was quite 'the man about town', dressed immaculately and with a large diamond ring on his pinkie. He was president of his Masonic Lodge and president of the firm's social club where he played 'solo' a card game at which he excelled, gaining the reputation of knowing what each player held in his hand by the end of the first round of play. He also had a lady friend, a Roman Catholic, much disapproved of by the family. It was well known that the two went on holiday to Whitley Bay each year and that a daughter by his companion's marriage was in the same class at school as Norma, his granddaughter. It was revealed that he had given gifts to this child, but not to his own family member which was roundly deplored. Sydney's sister, Ann, commanded the household with a firm hand. Each brother had to visit their brother, Bert now in Morningfield Hospital, a care home on the northern side of the city. Ann herself visited every Thursday bringing his favourite foods and making an array of clothes, including a sunhat to fit his over-large head. His blindness made him accurately sensitive to touch and when a newcomer arrived it was well to let him know that if Bert touched a dress or coat, he was just feeling the material so he could recall it, and on another visit not have to ask who had arrived.

This severely handicapped man had a keen sense of humour and an intelligence far beyond normal. He had been the boy who work out his mother's Co-Op dividend by calling amounts to his bedroom upstairs and he delivering the calculated amount back in next to no time. His brothers were allowed to bring outrageous items into the dining room, a motor cycle on one occasion, just to let Bert see how it worked. Before leaving for the South, I was able to bring David and girls to visit Bert. We sat in the sunshine all afternoon, chatting and laughing. Bert sent a carer for his bag of money to give the girls a half crown each.

A rift occurred between Ann and her brother, Alex, and they did not communicate although their homes were less than a mile apart. Norma was excluded from visiting, but Alec still left his offerings of fresh produce by the back gate. Most weekends he went to a farm at Cushnie, some miles from home, to help out or to shoot or fish or to his summer home near Balmoral.

Sydney had grown up well directed by Ann. He was relegated to the parlour each day for homework, and allowed little time to play with other boys. After sitting the entrance examination for Aberdeen Grammar School, then a fee-paying school, and receiving a bursary, his freedom was even more curtailed, except for visits to his brother at Morningfield. His uniform was pressed every night and he was the only one with a crease in his trousers!

Sydney's brother Bill was a success in the Royal Navy during the war, serving as an officer on H.M.S Gambia, which was sunk in Hull harbour with Ann shrieking in Aberdeen for Bill to jump; some strange sense must have communicated the danger to her. Most sailors in Aberdeen did not learn to swim, thinking that it would only prolong their death throes when far our in the cold and turbulent North Sea. Bill loved everything connected with the sea, and donated some artifacts from his time with his trading company to the local Maritime Museum. Nan, Bill's wife, came from a trawling family, meticulous in all she did 'a place for everything and everything in its place' was her motto, and carried to the extremes' was most people's opinion. Her choice was not to have children, but still she and Bill occupied a flat near to the fish market and harbour. People wondered that they did not aim to buy a house in a greener part of the city. Nan got a job in the local Post Office and announced that when they had saved enough money they would buy a house.

A mortgage was never to be entertained – that was getting into debt – you saved for what you wanted and paid for it. This was in spite of Bill having an excellent position in a thriving ocean supply company and having lived in a house in Ferryhill

Road purchased by his father with the aid of a loan from the Woolwich Building Society. Eventually they moved to a very nice property facing sports ground, not far from Forest Avenue.

From a distance, it was difficult to interpret this maelstrom of feeling and connections. Sydney was the link with everyone. He made it plain that he would visit his brother Alec and family, with whom he had a good raptor. Bill was rather tolerated than sought out, but he and Nan showed us hospitality from time to time. They felt it proper that his father should entertain his female friend in his home, something Ann was not prepared to countenance. They met together at Masonic Dinners. Perhaps Ann feared being ousted from her home, for which she had made so many sacrifices and invested so much of her life. Ann did marry late in life in the early nineteen fifties. During the war she had fallen in love with a Canadian Airman, who unfortunately was shot down and killed during a raid over Germany. Men of her age were returning from prisoner of war camps in Germany. The Gordon Highlanders had been captured at Saint Valerie at the beginning of the hostilities and amongst them Ann found an old acquaintance just returned and thought to be suffering from tuberculosis. Ann nursed him back to good health with nutritious food taken to his house each day. It was obvious they were an 'item' and in spite of opposition from her eldest brother that Bertie was riddled with TB, a wedding took place in Saint Clements Church, Footdee, bride dressed in white and given away by her smiling father. They made their home at Ferryhill Road, where Ann would be in charge of the household as always. Bertie had no claim to the house he was occupying. The situation did not please all members of the family who thought more input was needed from the husband, and that he should be the one providing a roof over their heads. It was widely believed that Father Cruden would leave his property to his three grandchildren. However, this was not the case when it was discovered some years later that

Ann had forestalled this by having the property signed over to her upon her marriage, but Bertie excluded from any claim. All was not peace and tranquillity when new furniture was brought into the home. Father remarked cynically as each old item was discarded and replaced with something up-to-date. 'What was wrong with that leather suite', or 'why get rid of that'. It did turn to Sydney's advantage in that my refusal of the brown suite while at Duthie Terrace, resulted in my father-in-law asking me to choose a gift for our new home. The big bay window called out for a centre piece and I chose a large pie-crust wine table in walnut wood, which has enhanced each house in turn.

Sydney's eldest brother Jim, was more adventurous than the others in the family. Upon leaving school he entered the grocery trade working for Collie's, a high class retail grocer with branches in Aberdeen, Cults and Ballater, and with Royal Patronage. His training was rigorous and exacting. Buying, stock and delivery soon became a way of life for the young man. His knowledge of his customers had to be wide ranging; which days they wished their orders to be delivered, what quantities of wine had to be sent and what substitutes could be send if an item was not available. This attention to detail stood Jim in good stead when he applied to be manager of The Atheneum, a first line restaurant at the east end of Union Street and patronised by the wealthy of the city, especially members of the various men's clubs. Never would one find a smudge on a glass or a piece of cutlery out of place. It was thus that Sydney found himself checked over regularly to make sure his nails were cut and clean, that his shoes were polished and his school uniform was hung up.

Jim's next more was to a tea plantation in Ceylon, now Sri Lanka. There he met some influential people and would never return to work in Aberdeen. Only photographs remain of his time in Ceylon and two brass crane birds which he sent home to his mother. At the beginning of the war in nineteen thirty nine, Jim was called for military service in the Army, where he quickly rose to be an Officer. Two brothers were now in the armed services, one in the Navy and the other in the Army. Alec's service to his country was in repairing and servicing vessels coming and going from Aberdeen harbour.

Post-war life found Jim managing a large restaurant in Piccadilly, Manchester. There he fell in love with his bride-to-be, the daughter and niece of the owners of the restaurant. This brought the first Connie into the Cruden family. She was Roman Catholic and fussy about protocol, especially regarding the one daughter who would make up their family. At the age of four the young lady was sent to a leading prep school in Blackpool where they now lived. After some time, Jim was dissatisfied with the rate of progress at the Catholic establishment and confronted the nuns with the observation "too much Holy Mary and not enough sums". Lessons changed drastically to a more rigorous programme, which was much more appreciated by most of the parents. Jim and his family holidayed each summer with his father and Ann, making visits to Bert at Morningfield. It was felt, in particular by Alec, that Jim's attention to Bert was rather meagre. He did not write to him, so that a letter could be read to him, and handing Bert a pound note did not quite fit the bill.

My frequent companionship with both my own family and Sydney's was drawing to a close. It was time to say my farewells to my own family and to the new one I had just become part of.

Sydney had arranged leave from work so that he could stay at his family home in Ferryhill Road, say his farewells and escort me and David on our journey to London. Once again I was to travel by sleeper. Jean, from Braemar, and her cousin in Barnet had housed Sydney during the past several weeks, while he scoured the newspapers for flats to rent. The northern area was chosen because trains ran into Kings Cross from Potters Bar, useful stations for work and journeys North. Upon my arrival a flat was reported for rent in a big house with ample grounds and a lake. Its description took me right back to Kindrochit Lodge in

Braemar and we could just afford it. The name of the mansion was Rydal Mount.

I was able to walk the distance between Barnet and Rydal Mount, so immediately took off on foot by myself. The mansion was owned by Dr Scharff and his wife, daughter of the founder of The Prudential Insurance Company. The advert stated 'a long let', by which it would overrun our intended stay, since we were interested in a house for sale which had just come on the market. Mrs Scharff was prepared to consider our request for just a six month stay, but would have to consult with her husband. Two people had already turned down the ground floor flat by considering it too far from the station and an approach drive which was too dark. I assured her that neither impediment would be a problem in our case. As a result of my visit, next day, Dr Scharff appeared at the door of our temporary home in Barnet asking to see 'a very persuasive young Scots lady'.

After a short interview and a cup of tea, an agreement was reached for a short stay of six months, with extension if required. I was very excited by this prospect. Mrs Scharff was kind and helpful. We were to occupy the Billiard Room flat of the magnificent country house of Rydal Mount, with its vast area of lawns and flower borders. It could be described as a farm, with its piggery and chickens. After Kindrochit, I felt so much at home and immediately entered into the life of this estate. Sydney could not quite understand my enthusiasm for our temporary home, putting it down to my relief at being united once again, but it was more than that. The Billiard Room flat was vast and on the ground floor. Its main room had a huge stone fireplace and logs would be brought each day at my request. At the far end, a window surrounded by seating looked out onto a flagged area with fish pond. Herbaceous borders full of colour flanked a centre lawn as far as some trees. Everywhere, there was a sense of space and freedom. One other flat, on the first floor was let to a very industrious lady who made blouses for some of the London stores. She was pleasant, but rarely seen; only the clicking of her sewing machine sounded from an open window.

Our offer for a semi-detached house in Potters Bar was accepted soon after our arrival at Rydal Mount, so it was expedient to have a removal of our household goods by The Shore Porters from Aberdeen to storage nearby.

Each morning, the gardener called to enquire which vegetables I wished to be delivered that day. We became good friends, he advising me what was best to have at the time. Flowers were his choice, and brought at his discretion. In appreciation, I weeded borders and cleared the fish pond of pond weed. The 'pig man's' two daughters had been longing for a baby brother and David filled the bill. Most days they came to take him to see their pigs. At just a year old, this was a great introduction to animal life. My only stipulation was that he was not removed from his pram unless by an adult. It was obvious from his muddy state that on several visits he had been released. A picture of a pig in his cloth book brought shrieks and waving of hands.

Our previous tenants and been Indian, and the kitchen smelt strongly of curry powder and strange spices. Mrs Scharff had thought of this and sent her cleaner to scrub out the cupboards and thoroughly clean out the cooker and its oven. Of course, I helped in the task and assured everyone that the cat could remain as part of the household, since he thought that this was his domain, having been much encouraged by the Indian couple. David was one year old and was to celebrate its passing by having a belated party. Mrs Scharff brought out a nineteenth century rocking horse which she had used. We tried David on its back, but he slid the three feet to the ground. The 'pig man's' daughters were invited and enjoyed the rocking horse. Sydney had taken a day's leave from the office and Auntie Jean arrived with her twin nieces from Barnet, to make up the party. Mrs Scharff's cook had made a sponge birthday cake. The one candle blew out in the breeze.

One other treasure was yet to be found – the lake. The gardener let me see the way through the hedge which led to the path surrounding the lake. It was a bit of a disappointment, in that a huge tree stump rose from the middle, and there was no sign of a burn feeding the lake, therefore no tinkling sound of water, no seat to sit and contemplate. Nevertheless, it was a wild place, full of bird song. At one time it had been used as a practice pond for family rowers, but now only wooden planks suggested its old use.

At the turning of the road going towards Rydal Mount, stood a very new building. It was the local Methodist Church. We knew that it had emerged from the Anglican tradition, but escaping from some of its liturgy. This would probably fit well with my Protestant beliefs and practices. Sydney felt much the same, so it was not long before we were attending that church each Sunday.

Doctor Scharff had written a book about the area around South Mimms and Potters Bar, pointing out both interesting and historic features. I was asked to proof read this document, part of which dealt with Queen Elizabeth's first journey from Hatfield House to London, upon her accession to the throne. Her entourage had halted at the old manor house nearby and continued to 'Dancers Hill'. There is no knowledge as to how the hill received its name. It is claimed that the first ever football match took place near Dancers Hill, with fifteen players on each side.

We did have friends and family to stay in this beautiful oasis. Our enormous bedroom had been Mrs Scharff's mother's silver room, where all her silver and ornaments were cleaned and polished every week.

The day came when contracts had to be exchanged for our new home at 66 Deepdene. This was not the happy prospect I had anticipated. Why were we leaving this roomy, comfortable home for a cramped house joined to another and sharing a driveway to the back gate! My head told me that it was prudent to buy the house; hadn't it been profitable to sell the one at Duthie Terrace.

Rydal Mount was to be sold in spite of my pleas against such a move. It gained a reprieve when their daughter required a temporary home, so did not reach the market right away. Mrs Scharff visited me in my new abode, cycling on her nineteen twenties bicycle to Deepdene, dog in the front basket. I was asked by a neighbour about my strange friend – was she a gypsy. I cannot remember if I answered that one.

Sydney and I decided we should have a 'house warming party', inviting the Scharff family, and near neighbours to make the number not more than ten guests. The conversations swung to innovations which had taken place in Potters Bar; the now efficient railway station, the development of Darkes Lane. Here Dr Scharff interceded, saying it used to be called Gipsy Lane, but no one could remember that name, which led to how long had each lived in Potters Bar. Only one neighbour had been born here. Mrs Scharff's response to the questions was that her family came here the day Mafeking was relieved, February, nineteen hundred. [Boer War]

Deepdene gave way to open ground to the west. It was in fact the last road in Potters Bar. To the West lay South Mimms, but first of all the busy Barnet Bypass. A stream ran through the open ground, where sometime cattle were put to graze. This, along with a large garden assuaged my desire to be out of doors a lot of the time. There was a row of local shops facing the main road, with a very good butcher, where some of my terms for cuts of beef diverged from local usage. I was asked what I meant by 'a gigot'. Some French terms had entered the Scottish language from its close relationship with the French.

On the far side of the main road, a footpath ran alongside the railway all the way to the station and a street with shops on both sides. This became a route we followed most days, David in his push chair and now able to walk home with the shopping where he had been sitting. The house was even smaller than I thought. Our stair carpet just squeezed between the sides of the staircase. The huge settee, purchased to fill a space at Duthie Terrace now overwhelmed our front room. It was obvious that down-sized furniture and carpets would be required. The pram, still occasionally used, could only sit in the dining room we didn't have a sideboard yet, so that fitted well. Each public room had a fireplace, nothing to compare with our previous ones, but both with all-round fireguards. That went well, until we noticed that David was adept at climbing, his little toes fitting into the strong mesh, so that he could throw toys or other objects into the fire. After one or two such incidents, I decided that fireguards were a danger. Another method would have to be tried; all explanations failed, so a cruel method had to be adopted. I took his little finger and pressed it with mine against the hot cradle. This did the trick. He decided that fire was 'bad' and 'tot'. Of course, I was chastised by the nurse/social worker on her next visit for removing the guards, although she could not give me a suitable alternative. The minute kitchen was just big enough to house the washing machine which I had just bought. The modern kitchen had a kitchen cabinet, and cupboards all round the walls at eye-level, an ancient gas cooker and an Ascot heater. Its door opened out on to a flagged area with raised flower bed and steps up to the drying green and upward slopping garden. The sight was uplifting, with its potential for further development. The patio made a useful adjunct to the tiny kitchen. With a long extension cable, I could do the ironing outside and leave pots and pans to soak there.

My neighbours were amiable and became good friends. Colin and Kerry, next door, approaching teenage, were particularly keen to have David join their games, although mostly to sit and watch. He was taken in when they thought fit. The family sharing the other half of the building were equally friendly. One grown-up son lost no opportunity for helping me carry shopping or going with something to the post box. Mrs Morton became my permanent baby sitter, having David often when he was too tired to come with me to the station to walk home with Sydney. Sydney was often gone for eleven hours each day and his only time spent with his little son had to be first thing in the morning.

David stood on the laundry basket, watching every move of his father's shaving and washing, then after a swift breakfast, they parted, waving their goodbyes. This also took place on Saturdays, when nearly all offices were operational until at least midday.

Three

Gardening had to commence with gusto. The flower bed next to the patio was a mass of Lily of the Valley, very pretty if kept within bounds, but it was spreading everywhere, so the whole bed had to be cleared. The garden path was nicely angled and we benefited from an explosion of colour from a border in the garden next door. Two trees and a low hedge shielded the top part of the garden, where a vegetable plot led to rows of raspberries, some quince, and blackcurrant bushes. It was a good place for a little boy to be invisible from the house. After some time a substantial swing was ordered for the rather small patch of lawn. It proved a great attraction for Colin, Kerry and myself. This was another learning curve for David. If he pushed the swing hard, he had to escape its return by stepping aside or lying flat on the ground, if necessary.

During the week David and I attending a meeting at the Methodist Church. Little ones where taken aside, during a talk for adults, to play games in another hall. One boy when asked did they have fun, remarked that they even had fat ladies who could chase you. Of course, it helped me to settle into this new community. Two other ladies were Scottish, from Glasgow, which made me feel more settled. Sunday was a day when we could attend church as a family. David had six pence for his collection and six pence to spend at the local newsagent. On one occasion when he lost one of his six pences, he was sure it was the one for church, the one left was definitely for the paper shop. And so, our lives progressed in Potters Bar, visiting family in Barnet by walking up Mimms Hall Road, bordered on both sides by cherry trees as far as the eye could see – a truly magnificent sight, even after blossom time. It was worth the five mile walk, just to climb this road. On Saturday and Sunday afternoons we explored the countryside, going to Hatfield House or Saint Albans.

It was quite odd to find people picnicking on the centre reservation of The Barnet bypass, when all around were woods and fields.

Once a month I went by train to London. It had become quite a ritual, after my visits to Warham and Gillows to choose the carpets and three piece suite required to replace the large pieces brought from Aberdeen. Swan and Edgars was the favourite stopping place for lunch, where the restaurant staff used to make off with David to entertain him and send him back, pockets bulging with sweets. Our visits to Rydal Mount continued until Dr Scharff and Mrs Scharff left on a world cruise. By the age of two, David had freedom to follow the gardener and visit the pigs, if someone could be found to take him to the stys. Inside the mansion, there were plenty things of interest, including a figure in a full suit of armour guarding the turn of the staircase, and with his visor open. Here any progress upstairs was halted, and careful eye kept on 'The Bad Man'. It was on one of these visits, that I was asked if I wanted David's name put forward for Charter House, a boarding school, where their son was educated. Naturally, I declined, not knowing where we might be in ten years time and questioning our ability to afford the fees. The question of schooling did crop up a couple of years later, when, as several mothers saw it, children were not to be instructed in good manners or told what to do. 'They had to be free to choose right from wrong', without knowing what that was. It did not resonate well with many parents, and one Welsh teacher advised me 'to get back to Scotland, where things are different'. Indeed that is what took place, because of a further government move.

I had attended a clinic for toddlers and pre-school children, which was run by a very sensible doctor. She was genuinely fond of children, and this was reciprocated. On arrival, girls ran to one side of the room, and boys to the other, where rows of chamber pots sat in holes in the walls. Round they went behind a screen and peed, sometimes with the help of mother, but soon on their own. It was deemed the easiest way for these young ones to become 'dry' at an early age. Dr Fraser was applauded for her help in potty training at time when nappies had to be washed every day.

At the time, my sister, Flora was leaving Dundee for the East end of London. She was pregnant with Kevan, and Bennie was now working near New Cross. They had no home at this time, so it was proposed that she came to live with me and Sydney until somewhere suitable was found in that area. This turned out to be Hither Green, as it happened, a suburb of New Cross. A feeling of loneliness which had been descending upon me since the house and garden became more organised, was quickly dispelled by the arrival of Flora. Together, we shared household chores and looked after David 'Aunt Fla' often preferred to mother. Our next door neighbours second son played skiffle music for us whenever he thought we were in earshot, and we clapped and sang in accompaniment. The Methodist minister made two calls to assure Flora that Barnet Hospital would be an excellent place to give birth. Upon asking David if he enjoyed playtime in the hall at church, he was given the reply 'you can run and big ladies chase you' with a demonstration of running away.

Kevan's birth was long and drawn out. Because of our association and Bennie's duties away from New Cross, I suffered association pains which would not disperse. I kept ringing the hospital for news, but none came until late in the evening a voice told me that a man had visited and would return next day. However, next day I decided to visit the hospital in the evening after Sydney came home from work. Kevan had arrived and Flora was tired, but well. She was desperate to leave 'this awful place' having been left in pain during the whole night. She declared, when help arrived in the morning, she swore at the staff and was anxious that this did not include mention of the nurse's ethnicity, which I gathered had been Caribbean. I put in an official complaint and received an interview with Matron, who was anxious to know if I was associated with the medical profession. Upon my reply of 'none at all' she said that Flora would be given a written apology for the poor care she had received and that better night cover would be put in place. This did, in no way detract from the joyous homecoming a week later. David was to have priority of his aunt for the first couple of days and we noticed no sign of resentment of the new addition to the household. Kevan was a 'good baby' sleeping well at night and crying little. He and Flora remained for another fortnight, before moving to Hither Green, on the other side of the city.

I was able to visit Hither Green on a couple of occasions, but Sydney was able to make the journey there several timea straight from work, and getting home late in the evening. He had to go – Flora had found a shop which sold oatmeal by quantity, so he came back with half a stone for our breakfasts. Because of my neighbour's kindness I was able to join a Scottish Country Dance club, just a mile away. It was quite common for me and Sydney to pass one another on the way, he to relieve Mrs Morton from baby sitting, and me to arrive in time at the club. By the age of three, David was a competent cyclist, discarding his balancing wheels and racing too fast to and from The Methodist Church, always too fast. His philosophy at the time was that, should an obstacle be in your path, you just jumped off, letting the bicycle go its own way; into a bush or tree at the side of the pavement. Fortunately, no serious damage was done to the bike, but it caused quite a bit of amusement for the adults.

One of our favourite walks was to Brookmans Park, a village some three miles from where we joined the path running by the railway, but going in the opposite direction from Potters Bar. A big attraction was the number of trains which zoomed past. The Cambridge Buffet Express was the favourite. For me, the interest lay on the other side of the line where there was a golf course; a Jewish one apparently and private. I had never come across such a thing, a golf course that was private! Farther along, two horses were usually in the field waiting for goodies we had brought them as a treat. One day David held out his gloved hand flat to give the sweet. Soon sweet and glove were disappearing into its mouth and shrieks of protest were coming from my son. It was not to be forgotten that the horse ate gloves. After a visit to his grandparents in Cults, the horse was address as, 'bloody horse' a term used all the time by their farming neighbour to both of his horses, which David visited every day if possible. They did not eat gloves.

On his return to Deepdene, David stood by the hedge at the front gate calling 'Hello man, Hello lady' as people passed along the pavement. It astonished me that so few responses came from these people. Apparently you had to know these people before a greeting could be exchanged. Another phenomenon struck me, and Mrs Scharff had the answer. Here people needed to know where they stood with regard to others, so that they could be revered or disregarded according to their wealth. Most people around us, it seemed were stretched to the limit of their financial resources, and it was considered unusual that we thought nothing of going to Aberdeen to attend a friend's funeral. At the time we were strapped for cash, but always there were resources to cope with an unexpected event such as a marriage or funeral in Scotland.

Sydney's father visited us and took David and me to choose lovely items from Swan and Edgar and toys from Hamley's, going home with Sydney after his day's work. Many members of both families came to stay with us in our new home, including my brother-in-law and his wife from Blackpool. They seemed to think our move from Duthie Terrace was a step up, away from the solid granite house with so much space to be filled. This time, the suggestion made was that we build out at the back of the house, maybe, my array of pots and pans drying outside on the patio area had been the inspiration. On one occasion, we brought my youngest sister back with us and was able to arrange for her return by sleeper in the care of the railway guard, who put her in a berth with two elderly ladies – quite an adventure for a twelve year old! Of course, my father was awaiting her return at Aberdeen Station. A cousin of my father's could come with her family from Bletchley to spend the day with us, and meet with Jean from Barnet. In no way could we feel cut off in Potters Bar.

Jean was a very willing baby sitter, and one lovely spring afternoon, I was able to catch the train for London and meet Sydney as he left the office. It was a magical evening, sunny and warm with no need for a coat or even jacket. My flimsy, floral dress with its broad royal blue sash was perfect for the occasion. We were to see a new musical called 'South Pacific', Jean's cousin had obtained tickets for us, she having some connection with the Dominion Theatre where it was being performed.

One more visit to London remained for David and me. It was getting towards Christmas and, as usual, we lunched in Swan and Edgar's and shopped in Hamley's. Dusk had fallen, as we emerged on to Regent Street, which was suddenly ablaze with twinkling lights. 'Is this fairyland?', enquired my small companion. Our last act was to leave a card of thanks at Swan and Edgar's for the restaurant staff who had been so helpful and friendly during out lunches with them.

Sydney's new post was to be in Edinburgh, and our move there was imminent. The visits to Rydal Mount had ceased when Dr and Mrs Scharff eventually embarked on their cruise around the world. Our stay in Potters Bar had been short, but still a feeling of regret at our leaving was quite pronounced. Colin and Kerry, David's older friends and neighbours, came more often to the garden and to help build mechano structures indoors. They were interested in finding Edinburgh on maps, and enquired about the journey there. Gradually, the idea of a visit to Edinburgh seemed a possibility for the boys, and upon sounding out parents, both parties were accepting of the idea that during the following summer my next door neighbour would bring both boys North.

66 Deepdene was on the market for two thousand pounds more than we had paid for it. Unlike Scotland, a price was usually expected below the asking price. A property agent handled the sale and charged a fee. An agreement could be made by the acceptance of an offer on the spot. A period of uncertainty for those involved existed until 'contracts' were signed by both seller and buyer, resulting in an unnecessary delay. Several candidates came to view our home and were suitably keen on placing an offer with the agent. For two, the house was too far from station and main shopping area. The successful candidate was a young London girl, whose father was a type-setter with one of the The Fleet Street newspapers. To start with, the agent was sceptical, wondering where the money was to come from. It came to light that the father was putting down one thousand pounds in cash, and his daughter was able to pay the remainder by some sort of mortgage, an unusual situation for a young woman at the time.

The Methodist Church friends provided a splendid tea in honour of our departure, and presented David with The Golden Book of The New Testament. I had learned that an organised removal paid off in time and worry. As before, our goods had to be divided into what we could safely put into store and items which might be required before our entry into the next property in Edinburgh.

In one respect, I was glad to be returning to Scotland. David was four and a half. Both Sydney and I were concerned about performance of schools in the area. One child had been refusing to attend school at the age of seven. The school wanted, 'to let him be', but I did see his mother chasing him into the playground; not a reassuring sight.

Pickfords the removal company, was our choice for the removal of goods. Curtains had to be taken down and washed, toys allocated to boxes, marked 'do not open'. A large box was allocated to kitchen items which were to stay in store. Drawers and wardrobes were stuffed with clean linen and clothes. China and glassware sat on the dining table, ready for packing by the removal company.

Once again I was congratulated on the organisation of the load by the removal men. Only the cat remained a problem. A neighbour who had said that she would have her, changed her mind, so unfortunately Sooty ended up in the care of a charity. Her first owner had confronted me asking for a fee that she paid to a vet to have her cat neutered. She did call at my door every day and entering the house at any opportunity. I refused to pay the fee and she responded with 'well have her anyway'. And so, she became part of our family. David was content that Sooty, like us, had to go and live in another place.

With our goodbyes said to our neighbours, and a firm assurance that some would come to Edinburgh, we made our way to a hotel in Russell Square, where we were to stay for two nights before boarding a sleeper for Scotland. Sydney had secured a flat in Edinburgh for us, while we hunted for a house to buy. London and Potters Bar would become just another memory for me.

It turned out that the boys would make the journey North by sleeper and together, in the care of the guard, and met by me at Waverley Station, Edinburgh.

The flat at number twelve, Whitehouse Loan, in the Bruntsfield area was the first floor of a large stone-built house. Once again, I had extensive space at my disposal. It could so easily have been part of Rydal Mount, with wide fireplaces and beautiful furniture. David immediately commandeered the space under the grand piano for his cars and books, which were brought to make him feel at home. Our landlady Miss Gibson, occupied the ground floor flat with her companion, Edith, also unmarried, and answering to her lady's every whim. It surprises me even now that a child living there would be welcome. It was obvious that his behaviour would be monitored, and adult behaviour expected. They were kindly in their way and, once settled David was much indulged by both fetching mail and delivering notes to the occupants on the top floor. They were two graduates carrying out experiments on chickens at the university. Sometimes we were invited for tea, when a lot of what they did was explained to us. Once we were taken to the laboratory where they worked and shown how blood was taken and examined. One cockerel ran to the equipment to have his blood taken, knowing what was to happen when the glass shutter was opened.

For David, the girls made a donkey with two heads, which in fact was a magnet, and David could not understand why the beast could eat with one head and not the other. One day the donkey was found under the piano, dismantled with only the head that grabbed the turnip with its bounty. As spring approached, Edith opened a door to a large cupboard in the entrance hall. It was here that all manner of equipment was stored and it was made plain to me that a spring clean was about to be carried out everywhere, and that I was expected to attend to this in my flat. A ladder could be taken upstairs to bring down the curtains, so that they could be cleaned or laundered. This was certainly a job for two people, so Sydney and I struggled to bring down these curtains, he at the top of the ladder to free them from their rings and hooks, a good ten feet from ground level. The main bedroom had two windows, and the smaller only one, but all the curtains were heavy. It was decided to have them all dry-cleaned, in case of repercussions over shrinkage, but this came with a cost we were not happy to pay, but felt there was no alternative. The bathroom was a delight, with walls of green and black marble tiles and almost the size of the smaller bedroom. Mirrors reflected light from each wall. Its spring clean was just a formality of what happened each week. The kitchen needed a lot more attention. It was modern, but had an old gas cooker. Again, cleaning took place each week. This time I was told that everything was to be brought from each cupboard, new paper laid on the shelves and everything washed and replaced in order. There were pots and pans galore and glass and china to support a household of ten.

Another cat came to join us as a visitor most days. He lived next door, but always returned home. The Methodist Church was within easy walking distance, and we attended it most Sundays. I mentioned that we would welcome any deprived children for tea and games. A church member suggested that I contact a council home for children made homeless by a break-up of their parents. Jenny and Margaret came one afternoon with some toys, because we had few. They loved the tea party, but it was hard to hear their situations. 'I don't have a daddy any more. It's daddy and Moira now and I can't live at home any more'

Flora had not been happy in Hither Green. Unlike me her neighbours were not friendly, Bennie was away a lot of the time. He was Irish, and a Roman Catholic. His priest persisted in calling on Flora, to persuade her to have Kevan brought up as a Roman Catholic, which she refused to do. She was beginning to feel that she had made a terrible mistake, and was not the one to capitulate on this matter of the baptism. Without Bennie's support, she wanted to return to Cults. The matter of contraception had become an issue. Her cousin had married and gone to Dublin, where she quickly produced seven children and was burdened with ill health and a large family. Once again, the spectre of a mixed marriage raised its head in the family. Flora returned to Scotland just before our departure for Edinburgh. Sydney and Benny saw her leave from Kings Cross Station one evening, the two men having an exchange of very cross words.

Colin and Kerry did make the journey to Edinburgh during their summer holidays. I telephoned to their parents from the station upon their arrival. It was a great boost for their sense of independence. We took them to museums and to Queensferry, to view the great railway bridge, and to the 'pitch and putt' at Bruntsfield where one of my shots was in line to hit a stained glass window of the facing church. All were shouting 'stop, stop' Cadbury's Chocolate House was a favourite stopping place on our tours along Princes Street. Edinburgh was 'sold 'as a great place to spend a holiday.

Thoughts of David's schooling had been hovering around for some time. A new bungalow at the top of Drumbrae was to be our next home, when constructed, sometime towards the end of September, nineteen sixty. Because of the number of new homes being completed around Corstorphine School. the intake soared to beyond an acceptable limit, so Sydney and I agreed that 'The Boys' High School 'or a 'Merchant Company ' school would be a better choice. The small boys were to be interviewed and speech and intelligence assessed. This was all quite fun, but David refused to believe that the racing car would go faster than the lorry. He tried to explain that at home his lorry outpaced the racing car, and so it proved here when put to the test.

Daniel Stewart's test was much the same as that for The Royal High, except that candidates were shown round the school. David's eyes lit up when he saw the room with 'ladders' on the walls', and asked were boys allowed to climb up there. I was much encouraged when it was observed to David of his navy blue trench coat 'you have a nice coat to wear to school'. An acceptance of the place offered was a mere formality. Life in Edinburgh was infinitely better than that of living near to London. The city was full of interest, from its array of shops on Princes Street and The High Street, to its port of Leith and the great hillock of Arthur's Seat with the loch half to its summit. Sydney arrived home from his office in Drumsheugh Gardens before five thirty, and was able to enjoy family life to its fullest. On a fine night, a picnic in the 'Gardens' became a distinct possibility before David's bedtime. Knowing that my time would be limited when we gained entry to number one 'o' seven Drumbrae, I squeezed in as many visits to museums as possible. The Museum of Antiquities, in Queen Street was the favourite. Daniel Stewarts College, where David had been accepted to start school, was a substantial building facing The Queensferry Road, with buses running between there and Drumbrae. All was fitting neatly together.

There would be no holiday this year, but a week was allocated for leisure time. This took us nearly every day to the open-air swimming pool at Portobello, just a few miles from the centre of the city. Food was eaten at The Chocolate House or at Jenners, the large department store in Princes Street. When asked had he been on holiday to Aberdeen, David's reply was 'no to Portobello this year'.

A church outing was announced to Rothesay, on the Isle of Mull. David followed maps and bus route assiduously from under the grand piano and was able to stand up and tell the group that, 'you have to get the number sixteen bus to Leith docks'. This drew gales of laughter, everyone knowing that a coach would take us to the west coast, where we would catch a ferry to the island. It did cause a debate, as to how far it would be by sea, going all the way round The Isle of Wight and up the west coast. School was not to commence until nineteenth of September. Although most Scottish schools had holidays from the end of June for six weeks. Merchant Company schools finished a month later and returned later.

There was a meeting to introduce parents and children to their teachers and headmaster. Tea was served while children played on the lawn in front of the school. There would be two classes;

twenty six boys in each. Miss Burt would be David's teacher and would continue with the same boys for three years. In this way, boys would settle down in school and become confident in their progress and duties. Miss Burt would always be there to talk to or complain to. It became obvious one Sports Day, the regard in which she was held, when two fellows now in their teens broke off their conversations to greet her and relate their present situations.

By the middle of September, our bungalow on Drumbrae was ready for occupation.

The doctor with whom we had registered came from Peterhead and seemed to be connected to Sydney's family in some sort of way. His wife, like me, was a McKenzie and two of our late mutual relatives had fought side by side at Gallipoli, in The Seaforth Highlanders. We had become good friends, and when the date for entry to our new home was announced, they were interested in taking over the tenancy of the flat. I warned Margaret about the spring clean and other rules. She was pregnant and wondered if there would be an obstacle to a child living in the flat. This was soon dispelled when I had a word with Miss Gibson, and she expressed pleasure, but would consult with Edith before it was settled, just a gesture of courtesy, without substance, I thought. In actual fact, it brought new life to the two elderly spinsters. The big pram occupied a corner of the Entrance Hall, with an armchair nearby, so that baby could be rocked or wheeled around before Margaret heard the cries and arrived to calm her child. No sound could reach the ground floor unless a door was opened, so in every way, the old ladies warmed to the newcomer.

During the summer, David became reliable enough to cross the open ground at Bruntsfield by himself to the row of shops on the main road. It usually took a long time. Dogs had to be stroked or a stick thrown to be catched. I often brought back 'a treat' if he had not accompanied me. On one occasion, I was brought back a 'treat' along with the newspaper. The money had been exact, and there was no note from the newsagent. My offer of payment for the bar of chocolate was refused because the assistants were so amused and thought it might be a ruse to get some free chocolate. Another duty taken over at Whitehouse Loan was for the lady next door. By standing at the entrance of her long driveway, he could signal when it was safe for her to drive out into the roadway. There seemed to be comings and goings all the time, so it was quite a big task.

A school uniform had to be purchased, and this was thought best to happen before the removal. A specialist shop quite nearby was where this could be done. Red socks were purchased, a dark navy blazer with school badge and red trimmings, plus a cap with badge and red trim completed the outfit. Other items could be purchased from a selection of shops on Princes Street or George Street. It was permitted that David could wear his kilt as part of his uniform, so my sister's kilt, a hand-down, was made suitable. This meant changing the flap from left to right, since it is different for male and female. Of course the tartan was McKenzie, a replica of one worn by a boy in another class.

Having checked the arrival of our new cupboards for the kitchen, and other details, a date was arranged for the deliveries to coincide, one from storage in Barnet, the other our personal effects from Whitehouse Loan. Having welcomed our friends into the flat, it was time to bid farewell to Miss Gibson and Edith. Continuing at Methodist Central Hall was possible, but difficult, and did not last for long. Only on special occasions did we attend worship there, but kept in touch with Sister Laura until she had to move on to another area.

Both Sydney and I were delighted with our latest home. The sitting room, with a large window to the front, reached through an arch to the dining area, also with a big window to the side; a modern feature at the time. Work was required on the property. A stone fireplace graced the sitting room, but the kitchen had to be fitted out by a contractor, on the recommendation of one of the building staff, in our case. It was said, to give the incoming owner freedom to make their individual choices. 'Crudens of Musselburgh' a building firm near Edinburgh, and much revered for its house-building skills, was rival to 'Hepburns' which had just completed our bungalow. So much fun was made of a 'Cruden ' living in a 'Hepburn' house, that we were awarded discount on items bought and installed by a number of firms.

It was immediately obvious, that new carpeting was required. Two carpets were useful in two of the three bedrooms. Curtains had to be abandoned. A new carpet running through the sitting room and dining area was ordered in a blue/green shade from Patrick Thomson's on the Bridges at sale time, with matching velvet curtains for both windows and across the archway, to be drawn on cold, wintry nights. Getting there, best describes our efforts at that time. Our next door neighbour turned out to be one of Sydney's colleagues, with his family. They were borderers from Langholm, Dumfries, a town very near to the border with England. A newly constructed clutch of houses is always a bleak sight. There was a low wall between the bungalows, so these gaps, left for the construction of garages were the only areas looking derelict. I relished this opportunity to turn this 'yard 'as I called it, into an oasis of greenery and colour. A wide, slab path ran from a wrought iron gate to the front entrance. Flower borders to the path were called for, with lawns on either side, and an evergreen bush planted in the middle of each. Within the year this area looked quite settled. The garden at the back of the house was almost square and needed a degree of imagination to rescue it from looking ordinary. Because of a slight slope towards a boundary fence at the far end, I decided it would be best served with a sunken lawn, but getting materials to make an edging around this lawn proved a problem. Sydney trenched the whole of the back garden over several months, and together, we brought parts level, leaving a considerable circle in the middle below its surround. Our ambition was to build a retaining wall inside the circle, probably with bricks. This was achieved when an advertisement appeared offering stone pieces from some local project. These were stone slab chippings of around six inches by eight, which could be built in the form of a dry stone dyke. Each day, stones were brought from the heap at the side of the house, from where they had been delivered, and built into a wall. Any visitor was invited to participate in this dirty task, which had become a daily chore. By grass-growing time it was complete; every stone had been used. After a layer of top soil had been added to the circle, grass seed was sown, and soon there was our sunken lawn, ready for its surrounding beds to be planted up and make a colourful sight. The swing, brought from Potters Bar was erected at the far end of the garden behind a Lawson Cypress tree, planted to obscure it from the lawn.

Reverend Donald visited us from Craigsbank Church of Scotland, and since this church was within easy walking distance from our new home, we became happy members. He was able to divulge to us that, as well as being our minister, he was also one of the governors of Daniel Stewarts College. In this new community, it was easy to make friends, and yet being on the main road, one did not feel enclosed. There was a choice of two lines of shops nearby; the one opposite our bungalow, had a very good butcher who was patronised from far and wide. The other row had a grocer.

Two towering blocks of council flats on the ground opposite, dwarfed the old-style bungalow right opposite, facing the main road. Towards the northern row of shops, and set back from the roadway, there were dwellings for elderly neighbours, with whom, June, my next-door neighbour, and I would become firm friends, indeed like family. Dr Cormack visited those residents on a quite regular basis, as did the nurse/social worker. Both made sure that if help was required, one or other of us would be on call to lend a hand. Mrs Campbell lived with her husband, who was severely restricted in his movements. They were members of Craigsbank Church, but only she was able to attend services. Her spare time was filled crafting items for the church bazaar, or for charity. Her big success was in crocheting intricate covers for toilet rolls. Money rolled in and it was said that they had even reached The Treasury. A relative was apparently an officer there. Her most immediate concern was with Professor Carstairs, an American who had arrived at the university, New College, and was proposing reform of our church's view on divorce and co-habiting. Mrs Campbells view was that this was a retrograde step and would result in a wife being deserted and left 'holding the baby' without proper support. His slogan was "Charity before Chastity". She knew a lot about both and her cry was 'Bairns will be having bairns' for someone else to look after'. Maybe some truth in her prediction. Perhaps this was unsympathetic to those wishing to separate, but at that time little provision was available for families who broke up, and society at large, considered this an encouragement for men to fail in their duties as a husband and provider. Mr Campbell never commented on the matter. His interest was in Chess or cribbage, which he played most days in the corner by the window with one of his cronies. Mrs Kilorn and her husband occupied the sheltered house next to the Campbells. Both were tall and slender, Mrs Kilorn with a hesitant air about her, never sure what her next move should be, but welcoming and mostly cheerful. Mr Kilorn did not enjoy good health and was rarely seen out and about. June and I were always 'on call' for these families. I was freer than June, who had two boys to look after, the elder not quite school age.

Another resident of the sheltered housing was a small man who was obviously the victim of an earlier stroke. His speech was slightly slurred when he was forced to speak to anyone, mostly a grunt and some nods of the head. The Forth Bridge was under construction, and of great interest to this man. Earlier in his life, it was said, he had been some sort of construction engineer. Most days, he was seen setting out or returning from Queensferry. Walking was obviously difficult for this man. He employed a kind of bouncing action, one leg pushing the other forward. Passers would ask him about the progress being made and he nodded enthusiastically. There was much excitement when work began on spinning the cables which would suspend the great bridge over the Firth of Forth, alongside its neighbour, the railway bridge. Crowds came at weekends to view progress and wonder at the elegance of the bridge, and that such slim cables could hold such a weight, made heavier by a stream of vehicles and at times buffeted by a strong gale. On one occasion we did catch up with this neighbour, toiling up the hill after his visit to Queensferry, but he signalled us to go ahead.

The opening of the bridge took place in nineteen sixty three and was acclaimed as a feat of modern construction and engineering. It meant that access to Edinburgh from the north would be so much easier. Instead of several miles by car, or embarking on the ferry, a car could be driven the short distance by bridge, at a small cost. North Queensferry and Delgaty Bay quickly became commuter places to live for people working in the city.

Mr Donald, our minister, was obviously fond of David and, as a governor of Daniel Stewarts, he relied on David for the rugby results and what was going on In junior school. I overheard the remark 'you have to have a concrete head to get into the rugby team'.

Miss Burt greeted her class each day when they lined up, doffing their caps as they entered the building. One pupil had lost his cap and was seen fleeing for the front gate, followed by his father in full academic robes and calling for his son's return. It caused quite a bit of amusement and subdued tittering before return of both father and son.

At the end of the first term, boys were allowed to travel by bus unaccompanied by a grown-up. Nonetheless, behaviour was to be impeccable, under the supervision of the conductor, who decided which young passengers were reliable enough to climb the stairs and sit quietly on the top deck. Most days, I could go to the top of Drumbrae and view any red and black images climbing upwards from the bus stop on the Queensferry Road. One boy peeled off lower down Drumbrae, even so, the climb could take half an hour. Dogs had to be petted and, should there be roadworks, every hole inspected before further progress.

Boys did not return home for lunch. Their school day was contracted, so that half an hour was laid aside for a full lunch, or just soup and a roll. It meant finishing early in the afternoon. Boys from farther afield could reach home in winter before darkness had fallen completely. This regime fitted well with me; gardening, or elderly neighbours in the morning, shopping or outings in the afternoons.

As building progressed in the erection of new homes in the road behind us, local children were attracted to the site after school, collecting unused cement which they used to continue where the builders had left off for the day. We adults did wonder if some walls were suspect when the house was completed. One boy had been given a ruler by the joiner and occupied the position of 'site manager'. He would not be parted from his gift, answering his mother 'you can't ask me to do that, I'm Ian, the joiner', when encouraged to leave the ruler somewhere safe. The workmen were not the only people to indulge these children. It was not uncommon to see six youngsters seated on Miss Smith's low wall outside her bungalow, waiting for some goodies to appear. Miss Smith had them dig holes for plants which they could plant and watch growing. Her word was law. This was Miss Smith's answer to the fact that her fiancé had been killed as the second world war came to its conclusion. Of course, she was bereft of the family she had hoped for, but her personality, good sense and kindness to those children, brought fun and happiness to all. By contrast, her sister, a paediatric doctor did not share this desire to be drawn into the lives of these children, who quickly sensed the different approach and stayed away when she was around.

Another project was placed before me by our minister, Mr Donald. He suggested that we, of Craigsbank Church become involved in supporting The Widowers' Children's Home. As the name suggests, this was a home purely for children who had lost their mother. The home was a large building, almost directly opposite the zoo on the main Edinburgh to Glasgow road. With some trepidation, I arranged a time to visit the home. Miss McCara, a tall friendly lady was mistress of the home. She began by introducing me to the two members of staff present, going on to describe her purpose in seeking outside participation. It became immediately obvious that she had everything well-ordered and that the children's progress and welfare topped her list of priorities. She explained that the children were not taken shopping; food arrived by van, and loaves of bread by the dozen. Fathers had neither the time nor know-how to bring about functions that are normal in a small household.

Questions were asked about my situation and experience with small children, other than with my son. Here, my encounter with children from 'Prevention of cruelty ' was taken up and of interest. Two little boys, Allan and Andrew were to visit me once a week for the day to begin with, subject to their father's consent. The following week, I would meet the two children, both below school age. Both told me that they were coming to my house to play games, both very shy at this point. I suggested that we walk along to The Post Office in Corstorphine, where we could post two letters. This was met with approval, and at The Post Office, I met a friend to whom I could introduce my new charges. By the time of my return to the Home, I was feeling that I had done the right thing and had something to offer the little boys.

Both David and Sydney were looking forward to the following

week, when Allan and Andrew would come to spend a whole day with us. David got out his cars and Lego, so that some toys would be on the floor, ready for play.

Four

At half past one Allan, Andrew and I climbed to the top of Drumbrae, where we could watch for David and his school friend getting to the foot. This time, there was no lingering. We were back home within half an hour, when I could hand over entertainment of the boys to my son. The afternoon went well, and the boys were returned home just after tea, most of Miss McCara's wishes having been accomplished. A line of boys greeted our return, waiting to enter Miss McCara's office, all with books and pencils in their hands. Each night, home work was checked by Miss McCara and comments made. She felt she could perform an important duty in the progress of the boys; 'It'll not be my fault if they don't all get good jobs'. As well as nurturing her young charges, this dedicated lady made sure that fathers were not left out. Sydney and I, along with directors of the 'home' were invited to meet those fathers willing to attend such a gathering. Both fathers of Allan and Andrew attended, and expressed their gratitude that we were taking an interest in their boys. Both homes were in run-down areas of Edinburgh. As meeting became quite frequent, it became easy to pass comment on progress. Allan was a particularly bright little boy in need of stimulation in any sphere. He enjoyed stories being read to him, but his Dad only brought sweets. Eventually, this father was persuaded to bring a book and join a library if he 'wanted to keep up with his son'. Astronomy opened up a new world for him and I was blamed for turning this man into an intellectual.

My neighbours were very supportive of what I was doing, arranging their coffee mornings to coincide with the days I had the boys. We sallied forth with a little gift for the hostess, often the drawing of a train; trains ran behind the Home. Quite often the elderly ladies from the opposite side of the road joined us, making the age range from three years to eighty.

Everything in our house or garden was regarded by the boys as theirs, only books and toys of David's that were put away were spoken of as belonging to him. When we got a puppy, Rex, it was their dog, as was the swing in the garden. This was most gratifying, and I hoped nothing would change the situation.

Some family members, particularly a Grandma, would be in a position to look after their grandson, and he would leave the Home.

The boys continued contact after going to school; Rex the corgi, would be lonely if they did not come to see him sometimes. Allan did leave the Home. His grandmother lived in one of the council blocks opposite our bungalow. I was not told the address, but found myself walking round the blocks in the hope of seeing Allan. I had asked the assistants in the paper shop, had they seen the boy I described. It was at this point that I realised my behaviour had become something of an obsession, and it came to a halt. It is hard to imagine the heartache felt when foster children have to be moved from their temporary home and friends.

Rex had come to us soon after the entry to our new home, Sydney and I agreeing that a small dog would be best in the relatively small garden. It would be a present to David, who seemed to favour the small, lively animals most. The evening newspaper announced corgi puppies for sale, three bitches and a male. Their home was in South Edinburgh, and we made arrangement to see them in person, all three of us. It would make a nice day out and we reinforced each other with the idea that should the dogs appear scruffy or badly nurtured, we would resist other charms. Our doubts proved completely unfounded; a rigorous check being carried out by the owner into how many children we had and whether our garden was fenced and would we have the appropriate vaccinations carried out in due time. Having passed the test, we were led to the back of a semi-detatched house, where a sleepy mother relaxed in a corner while her offspring charged around their small enclosure.

It was explained that the owner was not a breeder, but had wanted a puppy for his son. The others would be sold to suitable buyers. Fortunately the dog puppy kept running to David, as did the others, but he was the more persistent in his pursuit. After payment, the male puppy would be delivered to us by the son, next day. I thought the big basin would be a suitable bed for the puppy to start with, but we went straight to the pet shop to buy a new basket.

Excitement reigned, and it was agreed that the puppy would sleep in David's room on the first night, with paper placed on the floor in case of 'wees'.

'Rex is the dog's name because he is a great king,' David announced. This dog, indeed proved to be extraordinary in both learning and obedience. Most mornings, my first task was to clean out the baxi fire in the sitting room. I put papers on the hearth to receive the ashes for disposal to the compost heap. This morning, a puppy sat at my side watching my every move, and trotting behind me to the garden. Next morning when I had cleared breakfast, here was my puppy friend sitting by the hearth, waiting for the action of yesterday to be repeated. He was only weeks old. We were all anxious to take our puppy for a walk on his new leash, but he was to be quarantined for three weeks after his injections, in case of disease from meeting other dogs.

One of our first outings with Rex was one Sunday to Linlithgow, an historic town just north and west of Corstorphine, where we lived. We walked round the lake and viewed the Cathedral. Back on the main road, we wondered that Rex had not weed anywhere, and hoped that this would not occur on our journey home.

Gradually, we noticed a stream flowing along the gutter. It seemed never-ending. Rex already used a marked place in the garden, and although there was grass around the lake, he had only walked on the made-up paths. Linlithgow became defined by this rather mundane event.

Allan and Andrew took to Rex straightaway. They spoke of him as belonging to them, and bossed him all the time. When David returned from school one day, he asked why Rex was standing on the sledge in the garden. The sledge, in summer had some other uses, and he was there as 'outlook' from some story we had been reading and had not moved for over an hour. He certainly deserved all our praise and petting when he was told to 'stand down'. Our walks took us to Corstorphine Hill, directly to the south of Drumbrae. On top, it was an old wood of mixed conifers with birch trees around its edge. A tall tower topped the hill, and at times, it was possible to climb the steps inside. The view from the top of the tower was quite remarkable, and in turn, it was visible from far and wide.

On the hill there were dark holes and big boulders, with bracken everywhere. It could be secret and magical, with strange sounds, or it could be noisy, with dogs barking and children shouting as they swung out on trapezes attached to high branches. It held so much to be explored by a boy and a puppy.

The Sunday School picnic was looming, and excitement growing in the children of Craigsbank Church. It took the form of a coach trip to the outskirts of Edinburgh, beyond Colinton to a vast area of grass. There were races and other trials for a range of ages. Sun shone, ice cream melted and prizes were awarded to the winners. This, however, was not enough for the young participants. They wanted Olympic style stands to mark their prowess. It was fortunate, that Mr Donald knew of this new craze for third, second and first grading to be laid out. Two basins of similar height and two car tyres, one on top of the other were to be the platforms, the highest one covered in the yellow flag of Scotland. This was a really serious conclusion to the picnic, and followed in the same way the following year, and at private birthday parties, where competitions were part of the programme.

After three years, David's class were to leave Miss Burt. She had laid the foundations of learning and understanding amongst her boys. Each boy left with a diary from earliest years, made by herself with cardboard covers, containing at first pictures, and later items of interest in writing. This was not the conclusion of their attachment because Miss Burt's door was always open after lunch for boys to visit and tell her about their new life in another class.

Next came Miss Robertson, a lively lady, given to a very forthright manner of disciplining; the perfect follow-on to Miss Burt's nurturing of the boys. They were now expected to behave in a more adult and responsible fashion. A physically handicapped boy had joined the class and it was made clear to his classmates, that he was to join in their games at break-time and allowances made for his slowness and inaccuracies. Sometimes the pupil took advantage of this and boys stood round him pointing out his misdemeanour.

The zoo at Corstorphine came to be a back-stop for outings. We joined as a family and time spent there could be short, or in some cases all day. Soon David and his friend, Kenny, were allowed to go unaccompanied, walking down the long hill of Drumbrae or boarding a bus which stopped on the opposite side from the bungalow, and again at the entrance to the zoo. The large animals were not as interesting to the boys as the reptiles. The Reptile House had always to receive a visit, and the boys' knowledge of strange snakes and lizards far outweighed any piece of information we adults could add. One big attraction at that time was Alexander, a gorilla, who sat in a corner of his cage watching pictures moving on a screen opposite. He would nod to those passing by, until his screen was upgraded to a television, when he became engrossed in the new programmes. A parade of penguins took place each day at lunch time. A good half hour before starting time, Joey, would come to the pool's edge, and slowly be joined by the others. At a signal from the keeper, Joey would lead the company of little men in frock coats and white shirts to the far side where a meal of fish would be thrown into the water. For junior members of the Zoo lectures were given on various animals, their care and habits. It was interesting to have reviews of some lectures by the young members; their conclusions of the way monkeys just show off, and tigers can be so sneaky following their prey.

Edinburgh had so much to offer with its nearby Forth estuary at Cramond, its extinct volcano of Arthurs Seat, with the loch mid-way to its summit. To the west lay the wild country of the Pentland hills, and at Cramond a wide expanse of beach, also some shops. In front of several ancient white-washed houses a ferry could row passengers across the River Almond to Lord Roseberry's estate and along a footpath to South Queensferry. However, for boys bent on adventure, a tiny island sat out in the Forth, which could be reached at low tide, by a causeway built during the war to prevent submarines coming farther into the Firth. This consisted of huge blocks of concrete, broken down in places, but possible to negotiate. On the island David and Kenny waited patiently for the tide to return, when we would be 'marooned' on this Treasure Island. This was all very well if the sun shone, but must have been a worry if a storm blew up.

There were holes to be investigated, birds to be watched and creepy crawlies in the sand and bushes. A steady stream of shipping passed along to Rosyth, then we unloaded our binoculars from the back pack and viewed them close-up. It had to be a long stay until the tide went out again and we could return to the beach by the broken-down causeway. Such adventures were grist to the stories and compositions the boys would be expected to produce at school. Rex did not accompany us to the island but he was often on the beach, where he loved to be. He tolerated his crossing on the small open ferryboat and enjoyed our walk along the pathway to South Queensferry. Here was the great rail bridge, like a giant Lego construction, and alongside, the new bridge to carry cars, lorries, and all manner of road transport.

At weekends, we could be found with Sydney on the Pentland Hills. On one occasion, a rabbit ran out right in front of Rex. He naturally gave chase, and found himself careering down the steep slope of the hill, earth rising as he attempted to stop before reaching the foot, many hundreds of feet below. All we could do was sit by the path, watching our dog struggle uphill, along devious paths to re-join us at the top. Bus services were such that it was easy to get to Currie, a suburb of Edinburgh, walk across the hills to the south, ending on the main road near Hillend, where buses ran quite regularly to the city centre. Later, when David and Kenny were approaching eleven years, I fell in mud at the beginning of the hike. Tittering all the time the two boys, decided to walk behind me to hide my mishap from anyone coming up behind or looking backwards in passing. Some two miles into the walk, two ladies were approaching. I thought it looked a bit like Miss Burt from a distance, and that was soon confirmed, unknown to the boys guarding my back. Introductions and greetings exchanged, Miss Burt wanted to greet the boys who were forced from my back and now laughing, so that all had to be revealed and my muddy trousers commented on.

This was not the end of my troubles. Just after we had eaten our picnic, a big black cloud appeared overhead, and soon we were engulfed in a quite fearsome thunder storm. There was no shelter and rain soaked us completely. As often happens, eventually the sun broke through, and our clothes steamed as they dried off.

It was all downhill now, and we met a man toiling upwards. He gave us the bad news that the path was closed farther down, but that we could climb a fence and walk through a wood to the main road. 'What if we are lost' said Kenny 'and it is night?'. Then we find a nice big bush to sleep under until daylight. From then, it became an imaginary situation. Holes and bushes were assessed for their suitability as places to spend the night. Rex was reluctant to be man-handled over the fence, but together, we succeeded in lifting him over. If we did not find the main road, he was to be sent with a message on his collar to seek help. This did not become necessary, and we reached the main road without mishap.

Arriving in Edinburgh, meant that visits to and from family was easy. By boarding a train in Aberdeen, my two youngest sisters could be standing in Princes Street by ten o'clock in the morning, on a day trip to the city, ready for a tour of the museums and castle. Grandpa Cruden managed one visit to Drumbrae. It was late in the year, yet this stalwart of Aberdeen Harbour, with its icy blast from the sea, never felt cold. He slept with only one sheet covering him, and when I went to make his bed while he was shaving, I found it still warm.

In January, I had a strong feeling that all was not well in Aberdeen, so at the weekend, I boarded a train, sure that once again my father was ill. This proved not to be the case, and I thought my instinct had led me astray. However, I was to discover that my dear father-in-law had suffered a stroke and was housebound. He was tended by his daughter, Ann, who never left his side. No complaints about her restrictions at this time were ever voiced. She just sat there producing the most beautiful lace, embroidery and tatting, a slow and intricate form of lace-making. Grandpa died peacefully some six weeks later. It was nineteen sixty three. David was seven years old. He did not take well to his Grandfather being dead; he did not want him to be dead, and 'God was bad'. His funeral in Aberdeen attracted many family members, some even Sydney was unaware of, along with colleagues from the harbour and friends from his Masonic Lodge. It felt like the passing of an era. All three of us attended the funeral with my father representing my family, but he did not stay for the gathering afterwards. David would have a large souvenir of his grandfather. On a previous visit, he asked if there was a fiddle that he could have to keep. A search of the loft, reached by the hidden ladder against a wall, revealed no instrument amongst all the household equipment, seldom used, chairs, cushions sewing machine, and books. His Uncle Alec had played a fiddle and expected it to still be there. Downstairs, Grandpa had said to David 'will this piano do instead?'.

It had been usual for Grandpa to retire to the parlour on a Sunday afternoon and play by ear, the well-loved tunes popular at the time. My mother had the same skill of hearing a tune and being able to reproduce it without a music score. The piano was duly sent forth by Shore Porters to grace the wall of our dining area. A piano teacher had to be found, and this turned out to be a neighbour, a French lady, Mrs Geis, whose house was almost behind ours. A walk through a wide lane, took David to his piano teacher. Although Mrs Geis did put pupils through the hoops of exam grading, her main object was to instil in her pupils a love of music and a high degree of competence.

Because David arrived home from school early in the afternoon, he was one of the first to have his lesson. Mrs Geis had her young prodigies captivated, sending them home with paper upon which to write a tune which they could play for her at next lesson. Her mature students were full of praise for this tall, elegant French lady, who displayed so much imagination in her approach to piano playing.

Sydney inherited a few hundred pounds from his father. Ann had the house and effects. Any savings were divided between the brothers, with special arrangements for the support of Bert at Morningfield. It was thus, that we found ourselves able to bring forward some of our household plans. A new washing machine was required to replace the twin-tub. The choice was for one which washed linens at high temperature, spun them and brought the used hot water back up to be used for coloureds. It was a Parnall. Saving water was always an aim throughout my life, and this design had much appeal. A wardrobe was needed for the spare bedroom. The huge old-fashioned one which came from Duthie Terrace was ugly and clumsy, according to modern thought. However, in this I failed. A young man called, promoting the purchase of Chambers encyclopaedias, which I knew to be a terrific bargain and was glad to submit to the purchase. The main item bought from the legacy was a television of adequate screen size.

Early spring was not early along Deeside. Patches of ice still showed on the surface of water on shallow side pools on the river. Our focus turned towards the west of the country, but it would be summer before a decision was made to explore the Island of Arran.

Apart from visits to Aberdeen at weekends, our destination for summer breaks was to the west coast. We stayed in an hotel facing the sea at Brodick, the island's capital. Each morning fishing boats entered the small harbour to unload their overnight catches. Always, we had fish for breakfast. The routine became much the same for each visit. Brodick Castle lay just a short distance along the shore, and beckoned us. Goatfell, the highest mountain in the middle of the island was climbed. Glen Rosa had to be explored, with its woods and muddy bogs. Tragedy, on one occasion, was narrowly averted, when David wearing his Red Rothesay kilt had taken a path down to a pool far beneath us. Soon there were distress calls that he couldn't get out. Rushing down, it became obvious that he had landed on a bed of mud with water on its surface, which was reluctant to release its prisoner. I waded into the mud, but was of no help. Sydney became aware of the seriousness of our plight and brought branches to aid our escape from the clawing mud, now clinging to our legs.

Lamlash, a coastal village was within easy walking distance from our hotel, and Lochranza, in the north, which we found more interesting, were our regular destinations. There was, and still is, a regular bus service taking passengers round the island, with views seaward and stops at the whisky distilleries.

I had long sought a painting to be hung above the mantlepiece, and had visited exhibitions in search of an attractive landscape. In August, the Edinburgh Festival took place and local artists displayed their efforts on The Scotsman's Steps, an enclosed stairway leading up to the entrance of that newspaper's entrance. I was attracted to a notice which read

'Three Aberdeenshire Painters'. The three were; a fellow from Peterhead, displaying seascapes, Sybil Johnstone of Bieldside, next to Cults, and The Marquis of Huntly.

I entered The Scotsman office, where more samples of their work was on display. I did not want a coastal scene, so turned first to the paintings of Sybil's trees at a site just east of Cults. It was expressive of the area, but too dark and sinister for my liking. I, therefore turned to the Marquis's painting of 'The Lone Haugh', a painting of the river Dee near Aboyne, looking towards a heather clad hill, and with grass and a birch tree standing on the bank. It looked perfect, with blue water edged by white, crashing over some stones, the light green of the grass, and the delicacy of the birch tree. Without hesitation, this was my choice, and afterwards it was delivered to me in an elegant frame, and would grace the wall above the mantlepiece of all our future homes. It was much admired by our relatives and guests.

The Festival was beginning to be a significant part of Edinburgh's summer season, although mainly ignored by local residents. The Fringe was taking over spaces in halls, shops and cheap venues and was generally considered something for the low-brow. However, it grew year by year, giving a platform for many budding artists.

The Tattoo was always popular, and sold Scotland to the world. Some Australian guests were soaked to the skin one evening watching the performance, but along with Sydney and myself saw the performance to its close. At the end, it was the performers who cheered the depleted audience. Of course, it all ended with the evocative playing of the bagpipes by a lone piper on the battlements of the castle. Princes Street Gardens was usually quite crowded for the fireworks, bringing the Festival to its close, but pales into insignificance compared with present day numbers. To tell the time in Princes Street Gardens, there is a flower clock. It occupies a bank on one side of a row of steps leading to the lower level, which had once been The Nor' Loch before it had been drained. The clock is made up of hundreds of bedding plants surrounding a real clock. In spring men come with ladders and plants, to bring the scene to its colourful conclusion.

People like to stand by it to check that the time coincides with the boom of the gun fired from the castle ramparts each day at one o'clock. Sydney and David came to regard it as their civic duty to be wearing their kilts when visiting the Gardens in summer. It was a gesture to the many visitors from other nations, who, even in those early days attended the Festival. People asked to have a photograph taken of one or both in their kilts. Eventually, we started to ask where their home was. If English, we screwed up our noses, and laughed together. Many Americans left with photographs, as did many from The Commonwealth countries, whose family members had come to Britain during the war. One lady said her home was in Peru, a country which I aspired to visit, not knowing that that would be achieved some fifty years hence.

With our home complete with household items, shopping in town had become a real joy. Princes Street sported several department stores at this time, but my most used store for clothes was 'Patrick Thomson' on North Bridge, with a corner facing the High Street. All had restaurants with pristine white tablecloths, waitresses in black and white uniform, and in some, a three or four-piece band playing at lunch time. It was here, that some of David's classmates were brought to celebrate their birthdays. A room adjoining the restaurant could be booked for 'a sandwich and cake tea' after school. Games were arranged by the parents, but a supply of books, toys, and sit-down games were on display all around the room in the hope of a sale. There was a dais at one end big enough for three members of the band to sit, while they played for quarter of an hour before returning to the restaurant. Towards closing time of the restaurant, tables already draped, were set out in the hired room. Tea or squash was served, and at a signal from the host boy, sandwiches were attacked and demolished. At a further signal, cakes went the same way. A piece of cake wrapped in a paper napkin was placed by the plate of each guest. All stood up and sang 'For he's a jolly good fellow'.

Our birthday parties took place in the garden, August proving to be a good time of year. The request for 'a rugby party' was turned down on the grounds of injury and dirty clothes. It had to be football and Sydney and I with a new football and twelve boys crossed to the expanse of grass near the top of the hill. Markers were found for goal posts. The children were in play clothes, as requested. Sides were chosen according to surname initials, and off they charged.

We did see a few potential rugby tackles stopped in time. Half-time was a seat on the grass and squash or water. Back home, Rex greeted everyone enthusiastically. The boys had a set routine for these occasions, and I was unable to fathom the logic of where each had to sit. It had something to do with names. Again signals had to be observed and any spare sandwiches fed to Rex, as he waited hopefully under the table. Pancakes and sponge cake followed the signal given, and birthday cake was taken away to be eaten at home. On another occasion, the guests decided they did not want games, instead they would construct a coal mine in the garden by the swing, now Apollo 1. I supplied a garden fork and two spades. This would not last long, I was sure, and felt glad that we had arranged a treasure hunt with sweets hidden all over the garden. The boys toiled at their task, collecting earth from the hole in plant pots, and depositing it in the vegetable garden. James, from Fife, and in his kilt and flat on his his front, placed wooden struts around the hole so that it would not cave in. At the end of the operation, I cleaned the boys up and brushed down the kilt which was not 'play clothes'. The hole was almost two feet deep and eighteen inches in diameter. The search for sweets was dismissed, being left for those whose parents were later in collecting their son. The purpose of the operation never became clear, but it was obviously an enjoyable way to celebrate a boy's birthday. As it happened, the hole was in the right position to have a small evergreen planted to hide the view of 'Apollo' now displaying roadway light-holders and a huge cable drum left by telephone repair men. The boys had asked could they take away these items and it was granted. Rex was taken into 'space' after the Russians had sent a dog there.

Kevan, David's cousin, came with his grandfather to stay with us for a week, to be taken home sooner if he was not happy. Unfortunately, he had recently been diagnosed with diabetes. Type one or type two didn't seem significant then, but obviously type one in a child so young. He had become able to inject himself, with help apparently. This situation was new to Sydney and myself. Sydney was adept at helping anyone, having grown up alongside his blind and physically handicapped brother. Together, we offered bribes, comfort, even back home, although Grandpa had already left. I had the bright idea of seeking the chemist's help and he sold me a device which placed next the skin, just did the injection immediately. It was nothing like the normal injection tube.

Kevan would have none of it, and raced round the garden followed by me pleading for him to calm down. All of a sudden, he went indoors and I sat down to recover and think about my next move. After looking through the window in his bedroom where Sydney expected to see Kevan lying on his bed, he crept away saying 'he's in there with all his stuff out; doing it himself'. He appeared, announcing 'I can, do it myself, you see.' with a hint that my actions had been quite unnecessary.

The Zoo was of course, on the list of attractions, and David and Kenny set off with Kevan to show him all they had learned, and all they knew. Kevan was most interested in monkeys and chimpanzees, so the reptiles were given a miss this time. The week sped past with no wish to return sooner than planned. A further treat was in store for us when we boarded the train for Aberdeen on the homeward journey. An attendant came along the corridor as the train pulled out of the Station, allocating invitations to any passengers wishing afternoon tea in the restaurant. This was served with the grace and attention expected in the department stores of the city, and took up most of the time of the journey. The cousins were on best behaviour, and made conversation with the friendly and amused staff. It urged us to let David travel by himself to Aberdeen at the age of nine, when put in the care of railway staff. On one occasion, he was taken to see the great engine at full throttle. At each reunion, the cousins automatically joined forces as though they had never been apart. For a couple of years, they were 'The men from Uncle', a television programme for children. Their headquarters was in the outside washhouse by the back door at Fairview. Grandma was non too pleased by this arrangement and swept them forth with her besom [outside brush] something which was enjoyed and encouraged by her laughing grandsons. In Edinburgh, their mischief was mainly bent on raiding the larder. I had to pretend not to notice the odd scone or shortbread missing from a tin, and be sure there was something to be taken. It never got out of hand.

A year later, David was able to send a postcard describing his visits to his relatives in Aberdeen and Cults. He had been unfortunate in finding his Uncle Alec out when he called, and had to find his way back to Cults by himself. However, during the week his uncle had taken him to see the graves of his ancestors, of which we knew nothing, and told of Provost William Cruden, who lies beneath his flat table stone by Saint Nicholas Church [the mither kirk] on Union Street. The postcard concluded with '£ 1.96 --not a bad haul!'. It was common for people to give children sweets or money, but mostly money.

There was one event which put all of us at Fairview into a bit of a panic. The family had assembled for the funeral of a neighbour, leaving the young cousins with some other children, and a neighbour who could not attend the service. When the funeral party returned and the other children and the neighbour had departed, it was discovered that Kevan had devoured a whole box of chocolates by himself. We knew how to treat him should he require sugar. For one thing, David always carried a sugar lump in his pocket in case it was ever needed. The doctor was alerted and would come straightaway should any ill effects be noticed. Kevan was given a plate of porridge for tea; the answer to any ailment where whisky could not be administered.

An alternative to visiting the zoo was a visit to The Botanic Gardens, within easy reach by bus, and with the advantage that Rex could accompany us, but strictly on a lead and under control. The representations of giant tortoises found in the Galapagos islands were most intriguing, although fifty years ago not much interest was taken in their environment and habits. There were pools to be looked into, with gold fish swimming around, and plenty of space for a picnic near the heathers.

A car was an unnecessary adjunct to life in Edinburgh unless required for journeys to relatives or work. When Sydney's work with the Forestry Commission took him to offices in other parts of Scotland with his team of auditors, he was obliged to have a lift from one of his colleagues. This meant picking up and depositing him, which turned out to be very social. Because of the nature of the work, it did not attract married men with families. Sydney's work was based more in the office in Edinburgh, so that his absences were intermittent compared with others. Upon the team's return, I would have food prepared for all five. Sometimes they all stayed, sometimes not. Roger was a keen photographer taking slide pictures of views from hilltops, lochs and timber being cut down and transported in huge lorries. First of all, we bought an individual viewer, but finding that inadequate, invested in a screen and stand. So that an evening's viewing could take place, with David sitting by Roger, announcing the scenes and never forgetting any that had been shown before.

Craigsbank Church had a great deal to offer our family. The Wives Group was chaired by Miss Donald, the minister's sister, he being a bachelor at that time. We divided ourselves into small group areas, where baby-sitting, outings on the spur of the moment could take place, or a problem brought to the notice of our neighbouring members. All in our group were supportive of the elderly, and any hint of a coffee morning brought all to the venue. Sydney played badminton there and I became treasurer of the main Wives Group. Mr Donald pressed us to become Sunday School teachers. At first, both of us were reluctant, but so much was structured from guidance leaflets and themes for particular Sundays, that we felt we could be of use. It was fun being with the boys and girls each week, hearing their views and comments on the Bible, occasionally being astounded at the insight of the children. My class was mostly boys, Sydney's all boys. This division was common in Edinburgh, where over twenty five per cent of the capital's children were educated in fee-paying schools of a single sex. I had the feeling that I should be better informed on the history and theology of the Church of Scotland. I was given books to read, but when Edinburgh University announced its course in theology and church history, aimed at mature students, I decided to apply. The uptake was phenomenal, filling the hall to capacity at New College, the building facing down The Mound towards Princes Street and Gardens.

After the visit of Billy Graham to this country, there arose a wider interest in the teachings of the Bible, and Professor Carstair's ideas on divorce were widely discussed by both men and women. And so, I became engrossed in the happenings in the Early Church, its survival and progress, its martyrs, and early bishops. Even now, I cannot hear The Creed being spoken, without my mind saying 'Athanasius, 325 The council of Nicea'. One other person who wanted to teach Divinity at a school in the Borders, joined me from Craigsbank. Together we covered a fair bit before exams. Sydney was regaled with the contents of our studies, late into the evenings, when arguments arose, mainly about 'Free Will'; a hot subject, even today. Exams went well, sat in the huge hall at New College amongst a number of academics and lay people, who had degrees in other fields. Just as I was getting to grips with the contents of my course, Sydney was informed of his promotion, which would likely result in a move to the office in London. I had worked hard and had two exams under my belt, with only several months to complete the course and be able to teach in secondary schools. This had not been my motive in joining the class, as I wished to continue work in a voluntary manner. The value of this was brought home to me one morning when Mrs Campbell called, wanting my help in getting her husband from the chair in the bedroom to the one in the living room. Upon seeing my kitchen table strewn with Bible and loose papers, she withdrew full of apologies for disturbing my work. My thought was 'if I can't get up and make Mrs Campbell a cup of tea and listen to her woes, what's the use of all this'. The incident helped me greatly in coming to terms with any changes about to take place in our lives.

Sydney was a member of the Congregational Board of Craigsbank. It was not an onerous task, but did take up some evenings when refurbishments, and a new alter rail were to be put in place. Occasionally, Mr Donald hosted a dinner for board members and their wives at The Murrayfield Hotel, on the road leading to Glasgow. To some extent, it was a sounding board for the Elders, whose job it was to visit parishioners for whom they were responsible, issuing cards for their quarterly communion, and welcoming newcomers to the area. Church activities were well advertised through leaflets delivered to new houses upon completion and as a response, numbers were growing and a wider range of the generations was emerging. It was easy to feel settled and completely involved in the community.

David now had a master as teacher, who progressed his class in sport, music and writing. There was a class magazine produced, with articles and jokes written by the boys. David Wilkie, who became the Olympic swimmer, was president of the committee for one issue. [joke – a man asked what are the three sexes? Answer – male, female and insex]. Each page carried a similar schoolboy joke, often about rugby, never personal, but showing the innocence of the age.

June, my neighbour had a new baby boy. He was a placid, happy child who sat out in his pram on the front lawn, calling to all who passed along and anyone alighting from the bus. His social worker liked Andrew, wanting to check on his progress and June's management too often. In short she was a bit of a pest. June's two elder boys were perfectly normal and healthy. It ended in the young lady being told to cross the road and help Mrs Kilorn into her bath. The girl took the hint, and the elderly people on the other side, received the help and attention which had been lacking for quite some time.

Travelling from Edinburgh was easy. My Aunt had long moved from the Outer Hebrides to near Glasgow, and visits there were easy. My cousin's wedding took place there, a very 'kilted celebration'. Although living in a large flat, without a garden, just a drying green for clothes hanging to dry, and a day allocated for this, Mollie had a steady supply of fresh vegetables and fresh eggs. She had asked the railway company for a piece of their spare ground to be used as an allotment, which was granted if she fenced it.

There she planted all the usual winter greens and potatoes. The big culloch strutted around and his hens dropped eggs into the nesting boxes. As of tradition, David knew to kick some earth in his way if the culloch threatened a peck.

One friend remained amongst those who had attended the Methodist Church in Lothian Road. He was Derek, and lived in a flat on the top floor of a building overlooking The Meadows, an expanse of grass with paths criss-crossing it. It was certainly a climb to reach the final landing, where the boys greeted each other with a tussle. It seemed to be their way of showing affection. Derek went to George Heriots school, across The Meadows, near the Royal Infirmary. They were rivals in any inter-school sporting events, which caused great excitement at times, David having to make sure we were supporting his team. Another family had moved from the North of England, and were staunch Methodists, so there was little chance of their coming to Craigsbank. Like Sydney, Hugh was a civil servant and also a local preacher. Together with other friends, we had many gatherings, evenings both inside and out of doors, with games and competitions, and without a drop of alcohol. It came as a big surprise that so much fun could be had without the offer of a few drams or a glass of wine.

Going to the dentist presented no problems for David or myself. Mr Johnstone was an ex-pupil of Daniel Stewart's and required someone to report any rugby results. David was recruited, because his bus stop was right outside Mr Johnstone's surgery. To start with Mr Johnstone carried out a cursory examination of boys' teeth to gain their confidence for when treatment might be required. Thus, I knew nothing of an extraction which had taken place until my neighbour was telephoned to say David was about to leave and would I meet him on his way home. The extraction of one of my teeth, due to my encounter with a wrought iron gate one dark night, when the gate was usually left open, was not as daunting as expected, Mr Johnstone hummed a nice Scottish melody as he went about his task; most soothing to a client.

Turmoil arose in The Forestry Commission, as rumours of a new headquarters covering the whole of the country emerged. This would not take place for around ten years, but was unsettling for a lot of officers. Promotions took place before this planned disruption, bringing fears of "further movements of staff' within a short time.

Our next door neighbours, John and June and their three boys would be making their home in Inverness on John's promotion to that office. Sydney was posted to the office in Saville Row, London. So, once again we would be making out way south.

Fortunately, houses were selling at a premium in the area now that the contractor had completed his site. June was to leave first, and we laughed that our houses would fetch over three thousand pounds, and yet we were hard up at times for the odd pound. The boys had to be shielded from the confusion and worry of their parents, so an up-beat attitude was displayed on the surface, alongside facts which had to be explained. London posed no anxiety for me. I had decided to return to Potters Bar and resume life there where it had been left off. The only snag seemed to be a rumour of the new headquarters, and where that would be. Mr Bellis of Stewart's College was most helpful and encouraging about our move, advising us not to enter David for one of the schools that were unsupervised, and which abounded in the south, but rather find a grammer school with good credentials. As an afterthought he added the suggestion that we write to the County Council of the area where we bought a house, asking what educational facilities were in the area. As a last resort, David could return to his school in Edinburgh, where, boarding was now possible.

In early spring both men left for north and south. New neighbours occupied the bungalow next to ours, but knowing that our departure would be soon, we did not encourage a friendship to develop. They were an elderly couple, not given to much socialising, but pleasant in passing, and about to join Craigsbank Church.

By April it was time for our house to be put on the market. All expenses of the move would be reimbursed by the government, including any overnight stays at hotels. Sydney, along with others sent to the London office, chose to stay at The Ex-service men's Club. This was the only place their subsistence allowance would stretch to, and they were all ex-service men. It was congenial for these men separated from their families for several months.

News of the final decision of where the new office would be sited, filtered back and forth, Perth was a candidate for a bit, having lost an army facility, and was in the centre of a forest area. Maybe, our move would not be to the south of England, after all, but just up the road to Perth, a truly beautiful city set in beautiful surroundings. However this was rejected at Treasury level due to the inadequacy of transport links with the south. e g. no airport, and not near enough to Dundee or Glasgow. Chelmsford was a town considered, but that was also rejected by someone apparently wanting it to be nearer to his London Club.

Five

Basingstoke became the choice, since government policy was to have the office away from London. At this time, Basingstoke, like Eastleigh, was just a railway town with a good rail link to London, Waterloo. There were few facilities, not even a proper hospital, and very little in the way of decent housing. The office was a building next to The Park Prewitt Hospital for those in need of mental care.

Sydney was not able to participate in the sale of our bungalow on Drumbrae, most of the hard work being left to our solicitor, again a relative of Mr Gray from Ballater, and also a school friend of Sydney's from his days of hockey at Aberdeen Grammar School. Details of the sale were sent to local insurance companies and banks, as well as daily newspapers, with suitable times for viewing. As was expected, most viewers, came out of curiosity, rather than a desire to purchase. There were several offers below the asking price, which could be rejected. Kenny's mother had suggested that David play in her garden on one of the viewing days. I had just cleared the kitchen and placed some flowers on the sideboard, when the doorbell rang. Thinking it to be an early viewer, I opened the door in anticipation of a stranger. Those standing in front of me were far from strange. I knew all of them. They were relatives on an outing from Aberdeen. They were Ann and Bert, my in-laws, Bob Ross and his wife, along with a woman I had met once before. It was a miracle that all could fit into 'Susan', Bert's Morris Minor car. The friend, I gathered was not returning to Aberdeen with them, but continuing to Glasgow by train. They commandeered the dining table, putting gifts of biscuits and cakes there, in anticipation of the cups of tea they expected. It was thus that the first viewers were brought in to look over the bungalow. My apologies for my guests being a distraction, were waved aside, and Bob rose to escort them through the house and into the garden, all the time giving a running commentary on the newness of the house, its nearness to the bus stop, its unique garden etc., etc.. I was able to rescue the viewers and offer tea which was declined.

At four o'clock, I gave a big sigh of relief. Bob had escorted two more men and a woman around the house, none of whom was to make an offer unless the-price dropped.

My guests were preparing to depart, but not before David returned. He was able to tell them about Apollo and that it took a rate of seven miles per second to escape the earth's gravity, and that he had a secret in the ground that could send them off at that speed. Perhaps, that is why the mine was dug out at the birthday party.

After a week of showing people around the property, two candidates were anxious to buy, and prepared to offer more than the asking price. One was relocating from London, the other a retired banker and his wife, who lived in a large property quite near, with a big garden which was becoming a burden. It was also near to the Queensferry Road, which was becoming busier with traffic, now that the new bridge was opened. Mrs Crown-Hodge came on a few occasions to make sure of her choice. On each and every visit, her criticisms were comparisons with the home she was attempting to leave. Bedrooms were small, garden was small, swing was an eyesore, with which I agreed, but which would not be left behind. She visited the butcher's shop and the newsagent, to gauge the distance of each from the bungalow. She approved of David attending Daniel Stewart's College and left a bar of chocolate for him. My heart sank each time the red car drew to a halt outside the gate and Mr Crown-Hodge got out to help his wife from her passenger seat. He never accompanied her. By this time with all the criticisms, I was sure no offer would be on the table from them when our solicitor was due to open such offers on the appointed day. The couple from London were keen, but used to a different system of purchase, where an agent was involved to do most of the pre-legal work. They liked the Scottish system, where the deal was struck on a certain date, with no opportunity for gazumping or withdrawal before contracts were signed. Our solicitor favoured the Crown-Hodges, because they obviously had the money to make an outright purchase, and it was easy to establish their financial position. The only snag in the Scottish system, lay in the fact that an offer could be accepted where the purchaser could not come up with the payment either by mortgage or other means. At the moment off acceptance of the offer, the property belonged to the buyer to be handed over when all necessary paper work was completed. This situation hardly ever arose, because solicitors were vigilant in making sure a mortgage was in place, or some other means of payment guarantee, and placing a high rate of interest on default.

Three offers were on the table. The English couple put in an offer just approaching the asking price, as was usual in the south. The two other offers went far beyond asking price, and it went to Mr Crown-Hodge, the retired banker. In the space of ten years, Sydney and I had bought and sold three very different properties.

A sad event took place in the selling of the bungalow. On the Monday after the opening of the offers, a very elderly lady called to ask if she could view the property, and I had to tell her that it had just been sold. She was Lady Grove, and had been in a nursing home for two years, with her furniture in store and her car in a friend's garage at Cramond. She too, wanted to be near shops and public transport. She had been willing to pay well over the asking price, but too late. The only thing I could do was to alert neighbours and friends from church to advise her of any bungalows up for sale, particularly on the bus route. Some time later, we were informed that she had been successful in finding a home near her friend.

Just before Sydney left, Craigsbank had a visit from the newly appointed Moderator of the Church of Scotland This appointment lasted for one year only, so that the honour could not be abused in any way. It meant a very busy year for the recipient, and the congregation felt very grateful and privileged to have him preach to us. I was invited to read a short passage from the Bible, and later explain the work done by the Wives' Group. I spoke about the boys, Allan and Andrew and the need for pre-school children to experience life in a small, family situation. Mr Donald emphasized the work done for the elderly on Drumbrae, but the group regarded this, not as a project, but merely being neighbourly.

Miss McCara of the boys' home, arranged a farewell party one Saturday for me and David. Rex was included and proved popular, being taken to the playground and along the pavement. Both fathers were there, and were able to tell me how their lives were progressing, and their hopes for their sons. Allan was doing well at school, as I was sure he would, and was happy in his surroundings with his grandmother, who I now learned was his maternal grandmother. Although sad, I was able to leave with a certain amount of comfort that all would be well with the boys.

David's farewells were another matter. It was difficult to gauge what information would be helpful, and what distressing. He was aware that he would be leaving' Stewart's and starting at another school, a fact received but the implications not fully understood. Saying 'goodbye to the boys' and Miss Burt was going to be difficult, and maybe upsetting. Sydney and I decided that leaving at the end of the school session would mitigate some of this hardship, and schools in England started later for their winter session.

After one month, Sydney was back in Edinburgh on his government warrant and had some annual leave at home. The new occupiers weren't anxious to have possession of the bungalow, so time could be spent planning our move in an orderly fashion. David's small red bike was sold, along with unwanted items of furniture. Sydney, along with some other colleagues had secured a house on a new estate at Harestock, Winchester. As said before, Basingstoke would not be home for any of the transferred staff. Some chose villages near to Basinstoke, like Tadley and Old Basing, which had quite a history. Winchester appealed to me. Its history was well known and I could look forward to visiting its castle, its Cathedral and its surrounding countryside. It became quite a focus for David, he being soaked in the events of Robert The Bruce and Stirling Castle.

Time allowed us to leave at a leisurely pace, making last visits to The Gardens and to Arthurs Seat, with its views all over the Edinburgh which we had grown to love. Help came from all quarters to make our move to the south smooth. A neighbour, from behind the bungalow called to say 'remember, if you want your bagpipes taken down from the loft, I'm your man'! Mrs Geis was moving back to France, or having a long holiday there, so that her final lessons for all her pupils were before Easter. David came home with sheets of music paper on which to write tunes. Kenny and friends who lived in the road behind our home were depressed at losing, first the boys next door and soon David. Only occasionally, did they sit on Miss Smith's low wall waiting for the invitation to partake of biscuits and squash. Now they played the odd game of football in the roadway, which was safe until six o'clock when people returned from work.

Mrs Kilorn and Mrs Campbell came together to say their farewells, well before we had a date for the removal. They had bought me a pale yellow under slip as a parting gift, which later became the butt of a joke. Both Allan and Andrew's fathers sent letters via Miss McCara with best wishes for all our futures. With one letter came a neat parcel, and inside lay a satin slip, exactly the same as the ladies had brought earlier.

All sort of speculation arose from this gift amongst my friends, and I did wonder had it been bought for a deceased wife, in which case it was even more rewarding. I was most touched by these gestures of thanks and good wishes.

While Sydney was at home and about to return south, I heard a sound like a drip, drip around the dining area. As I walked through the archway, a big drop of water hit my head, 'a flood, a flood' I screamed, as further drops fell. Sydney went straight for the stopcock to turn off the water supply. He moved to separate the adjoining carpets, under the arch with 'move out of my way, I can't stop to comfort you now'. I was of some use, fetching the stepladder from the cupboard in the hall, part of which contained bedding and clothes. I could see that water was running down a pipe and soaking the linen. Sydney fetched a basin and was able to punch a hole in the ceiling above the arch, so that a rush of water fell into the basin and other receptacles. This meant that our only supply of water was from the tank, until a plumber could make a repair. The loft was saturated, of course, but its clearing and drying out was for another day. With good luck, most of the linen in the cupboard had been taken to the spare bedroom in readiness for packing.

The bungalow had a ten year guarantee on any faults, and the faulty connection joining a pipe to the main water supply had been a danger for years. Half of the ring was intact, but half was dirty and had never been properly attached. A plumber was sent by Hepburns, the construction company, the following day to repair the fault and look over the water supply. Again the office staff were amused by the fact that a Cruden was living in a Hepburn house, 'Crudens', being the huge construction firm based in Musselburgh, near Edinburgh, and well known throughout the area. Our solicitor was informed of the repair, and no doubt, passed the information to our buyer. We did, however, receive compensation from the builder, although not sought, and the offer of discount on any services in future.

All the family from Aberdeen paid us farewell visits. My parents came, but only stayed one night. My sisters came for the day, but spent it in Edinburgh, coming home in time to see David, have some tea, and catch their train back to Aberdeen. Glasgow was not left out, but only my aunt, Mollie, stayed over. Sydney's niece, Norma, was now married and living in East Kilbride, near Glasgow, but only her husband visited, he being employed by S.T.C. [Standard telephones and Cables], a firm at the cutting edge of new technology, and frequently called to Edinburgh.

Mr Bellis, David's schoolmaster had given me good advice to contact Hampshire County Council about education in the county. Upon my enquiry, a comprehensive booklet was sent by the Education Department, outlining all the secondary schools around Winchester. The percentage of pupils attending Grammar Schools was 20%, and the number of boys gaining places at university was quoted. Peter Symonds Grammar School for boys seemed a good follow-on from Daniel Stewarts College. Its rules were laid out alongside the curriculum and choice of subjects. There were no school fees! Before the official eleven-plus examination was announced, mock papers were sent round schools, giving pupils the opportunity to gauge time to answer questions and get used to exam techniques. It all seemed forward thinking. Daniel Stewarts College received these papers and set them to both classes of eleven year old boys. Every boy passed, I was told. Their English had been helped, no doubt by the fact that they had been studying Latin for several months, and that their spelling game was to find words in the Scotsman newspaper for a quiz. This developed into a competition to find words there which boys thought no one else would be able to spell. Classes were to be changed from the cleverer boys being classed 'A' pupils. The letters were reversed to avoid any feeling of inferiority amongst the less able. Boys soon reversed this connotation, by their label of 'B' for brains and 'A' for asses.

The government allowed a preliminary visit by wives to see their new home. David, and I boarded the train, bound for Kings Cross and Winchester, Rex being left behind with a neighbour. The main object of our visit was to choose fireplace, kitchen units, and heating system. We were to stay in The God Begot hotel on the High Street and visit the estate agent selling the house we had selected in Abbots Ann Road, Winchester. It was still at first floor level, but looked promising and nicely positioned towards the end of a cul-de-sac.

Although now early April, the wind blew and the air was very cold. The builder's office was at Winnall, a new industrial site on the north side of Winchester. The three of us set off, clad in raincoats, up Water Lane and now in a blizzard. Snow was not expected so far south, at almost any time of the year, certainly not in April. A fire glowed in the office where our choices were to be made. The staff were kind and attentive, offering tea or coffee, and a chair by the fire. Choices made, we were glad to return to the comfort of our hotel in The High Street.

This ancient building right across and alley from the 'Royal Oak', the oldest pub in England, had all the hallmarks of its medieval past. Its bedrooms were named after early Kings; Edgar, Aethelred, even Cnut, and of course, Alfred. The wooden passages sloped towards heavy doors of the small rooms. Again, a wood fire blazed in the wide hearth, in the hallway where three wine tables sat near a long bench, skirting one wall. A small dining area lay to one side of a wide, oak staircase leading to our bedrooms on the upper floor. All was cosy and compact.

David was entranced by the dates of these kings, comparing the times of their reigns with those of the earliest Scottish ones, Malcolm Canmore, with his shooting castle in Braemar and Kenneth McAlpine. Next day Winchester burst upon us all. Its ancient history, its ancient buildings, gateways and waterways, took our breath away. David was first to explore. The scaffy [road sweeper, in English] passed the time of day with him, pointing him across the road towards the Cathedral. He became the first person to show us Winchester Cathedral in all its splendour.

The High Street, after nine o'clock was busy with traffic, servicing the department stores and smaller shopping outlets. My greeting at Woolworths was 'good morning, would you care for something from this counter?', a pleasant change from 'hallo hen, whit ye want?' in the Edinburgh store. This city had taken us all by storm, and David and I thanked and praised Sydney for selecting this place to be our new home.

Back in Edinburgh, Mr Crown-Hodge had indicated a date for entry which did not coincide with the likely completion of our new house, so it was necessary for a temporary home to be found. The first agent to be approached was Maurice Beale, whose office was at the top of the High Street. During a conversation with him later, it transpired that he was the brother of Dr Jean one of our doctors in Cults, who we knew so well.

One flat up for rent seemed suitable. It was in Saint Cross, a fair walk to the station, and Sydney didn't have his bicycle any more. He did not plan to have a new car until our move was complete. There were two snags to this rental; first a long lease was hoped for by the owner, and secondly, we had a dog. All three of us were adamant that Rex would be with us. This dampened our spirits somewhat, but fuelled our resolve to find somewhere on this visit. Other possibilities were either too expensive or too far from the railway station. It would be left for Sydney to find us a place, perhaps in Basingstoke itself, for the few months remaining before our move to Abbots Ann Road. However, the matter was resolved by the owner who was fond of dogs, had one old fellow living with her, without objection. She had kindly consulted with five other owners of flats who were agreeable to having the animal for the short time. There was no further mention regarding length of rental, and Sydney signed up for a six month period. We now felt free to enjoy the sights and experiences of this ancient Cathedral city.

It came as a relief that so much had been settled for our future, in particular, that our son had found so much to enjoy in Winchester, and was looking forward to life here. We could not have been more wrong. One month hence we would be living in our new temporary home in Saint Cross, with our goods in store and Rex with us.

Prize-giving for Stewart's pupils took place in The Usher Hall in Edinburgh, and we were just in time to attend this event when Sydney returned from one of his duties outside the city. The Hall was packed with boys, parents and grandparents The usual speeches were made, a new head boy was announced, and school musicians entertained the audience. Afterwards, several boys and parents retired to The Chocolate House for refreshment.

During what turned out to be our last visit to The Gardens, David and I were discussing the incarceration of Stewart of Appin in a cell in Edinburgh Castle, just above us. High on the castle rock, we could see the little postern window from which he had made his bold escape. Foolishly, I said, 'shall we go up as far as we can?'. Without delay, we went round to the side of the rock facing Lothian Road and found a path of sorts going upwards. I was in my city clothes, black suit with white flecks, and red hat. The climb was easy to start with, becoming rougher and strewn with boulders, the farther up we went. One last effort, and we would reach a flat stone where we both could sit and have a view of The Gardens and look upwards to see how near we were to the barred window above.

As I strove for a foothold to reach this small platform above, a searing pain struck my left leg, making me scream out. The narrow path at that point was just level enough to save me from falling farther down the rock. Any idea of reaching the postern window had to be abandoned for small, painful steps towards The Gardens. Somehow, David got me to the bus stop and home. Because of our imminent departure from Edinburgh, I could not take the advice of my friend and doctor to be in hospital, more than likely having an operation on my Achilles tendon. My recourse for treatment had to be the local pharmacist who shored the leg and knee up with firm bandaging. However could I manage the removal, hobbling around like this was my question. My aim had been to leave the bungalow in pristine condition for the next occupant; windows clean and sparkling, paths clear of any weeds and my artifacts brought to the spare bedroom to be laid out in order for when the removal men arrived. Help arrived in the shape of Mrs Gillam, a lady from the block of flats opposite, who had been suggested to me by a church member. The short term work suited Mrs Gillam, as she was hoping to have work cleaning a bank. Before long, I could see how meticulous and versatile this lady could be. She took preparations for the removal into her own hands, washing and selecting items for relay to the spare bedroom, and refusing to sit for a break, when my friends called. My last memory of Mrs Gillam was of this tall lady on the opposite side of Drumbrae, followed by my husband, attempting to return the cardigan which she had left behind.

Sydney left after his few days leave from work to supervise the removal, and David and I with bags packed and keys handed over to the new owner, retired with Rex to a small hotel in the Haymarket district of Edinburgh. Our room was small and basic. Twin beds occupied most of the space, and Mrs Gillam would have blanched at the sight of the shower room. However, there was a wash basin. As we left after our first breakfast, we were passed by five stalwart 'Vikings 'completely naked, who nodded a greeting. They were part of a team of rowers, about to compete somewhere on the west coast.

David had said his farewells at school some time before to Miss Burt, and his other teachers, to Mr Bellis, his headmaster, and the boys he would not be joining the following term. It was easy for me to think he had taken it all in his stride. However, on the second night of our stay at the hotel, he became very angry, saying he had never been consulted about the move and that he did not want to leave Edinburgh and Daniel Stewarts College. The whole episode came as a shock to me. I thought he'd been gradually guided through the process of our move. I could take some comfort from the fact that Stewarts was to open a boarding house, and that he could continue there should he not settle in Winchester. By next morning the mood had changed, and together, we were looking forward to our long journey by train. Our sleeper was booked, our luggage in 'left luggage', and we were free to walk along Princes Street. I watched David on the putting green, although inhibited by my leg, we made a final visit to The Chocolate House, and ate high tea in an hotel near to the railway station. The sleeper train did not leave until later in the evening, but we were able to board any time after seven o'clock. It was a carriage for four passengers, but because of the dog we were able to have it to ourselves. It later transpired that this coach had been added on. By eight o'clock David was undressed and reading a book on the top bunk, Rex was asleep underneath the spare bed. The train left on time and soon all three of us were fast asleep. It was quite a rough night. Trees were being buffeted and I awoke to the terrible swinging from side to side of our compartment. It was then that I heard a voice from the top bunk saying 'I feel sick'. I found the pot in the cupboard beneath the wash basin, and handed it up to the top bunk. The disturbance woke Rex who poked his nose out from beneath the bed to find the pot from above landing in front of him. He was too stunned to bark and retreated to safety in the far corner of his sleeping quarters, only emitting a whining sound from time to time. The train had few stops, but each time it started up again, our compartment felt as though it would break free and we would be stranded somewhere in the north of England.

Sydney was able to meet us when we landed, so to speak, and help with our luggage to our destination of Winchester, Hampshire. Once again, we would spend nights in The God Begot Hotel, welcomed by Flight Lieutenant Wilson and his wife, who already occupied a house where ours was under construction.

My first port of call was to Dr Gibson, whose practice was in Southgate Street, just opposite Saint Thomas Church. The cause of my injury was dragged from me, resulting in shaking of the head, and loud laughter. Options set in front of me were to wait about ten days to be seen at Winchester Hospital, or he could send Miss Seymour, the physiotherapist to the Southampton football players, on Monday. It was already Friday, and because of the delay in treatment, my leg had shrunk to almost half its usual circumference.

Six

Our temporary luggage, including David's bicycle, had arrived at the flat and we had been greeted by Miss Rafferty, a formidable neighbour with a liking for small dogs of intelligence. On Monday morning Miss Seymour duly arrived and proved pivotal in getting me back on my feet. She was not hopeful to begin with that an operation would not be the answer. Her regime of exercises were to be performed five times a day for a few days. However, I decided that they would be performed each hour. Well do I remember standing at the window of flat No 4 'The Normans' looking out onto the colourful bed of flowers below, and stretching up and down. At next visit, it was decided that exercises would proceed for one more day, including massage with a big, black instrument, and if no movement was felt, my repair would be carried out in hospital. At the last gasp a small movement was felt, and I was really on the road to recovery. Any effort was welcomed gratefully, it being up to me now. Miss Seymour's daily visits were to be greatly missed. She was of Hampshire and knew each town and village. The history of the county was her hobby, and each day she had further details to impart of ancient routes and how pubs had come by their names. It became our hobby to seek out the unusual pathways, mainly to churches. Miraculously, after just a fortnight, my leg had regained its previous proportions, and I was walking along Kingsgate Road to town.

Our first real expedition took us up Mead Road at Saint Cross, over the railway line and on on to a pathway leading upwards to The Yew Tree, an ancient landmark, from where another path led downhill to Compton and Otterbourne. On the first occasion we caught a bus home from there. Saint Catherine's Hill became the object of a daily race to its top and down again; the dog did need exercise! At other times, a walk by one of the tributaries of the Itchen was our route. So long ago, even the smaller streams had fish swimming around. It was never long before one appeared in the clear chalk water. Cray fish were to be seen at an outlet of an overflow, going under the roadway.

This area, with its rivers, its water meadows, and wildlife was of constant interest. The chapel of Saint Cross was a short distance away, with its ancient buildings, housing The Brothers of Saint Cross, a charity set up to house elderly men. It had also provided food for one hundred men each day in the apt named 'Hundred Men's Hall', just inside the entrance gateway. This hall is much in use throughout part of the year as a cafe' for passing holiday-makers interested in this historic way of life. This enterprise is run entirely by volunteers for 'The Friends of Saint Cross'. At the Porter Lodge, one can ask for 'The Wayfarer's Dole', a measure of beer and a piece of bread, given to any traveller.

Looking from a bridge over the Ichen Navigation River, the imagination brings life to the ancient ships, plying their way to Winchester and plunder. Winchester bears the ancient name, Wenta Belgarum, after the settlement on the top of Saint Catherine's Hill, with its rampart and ditch running round its edge, to ward off would-be attackers. It was not long before we discovered a swimming pool on one of the rivers. Part of the river was blocked off for this purpose; no heating, no changing rooms and hardly a walkway, other than a narrow path. Shrieks of laughter came to the roadway from children enjoying themselves in the river, David always amongst them. Sometime during the nineteen sixties, this amenity was closed down in the interests of hygiene and safety. The Lido, just off the Andover Road, and still in Winchester, was the replacement and met with all the regulations of health and safety current at the time.

Although staunchly Presbyterian, we followed my grandmother's example of sharing worship with other denominations. Our own wish was to become part of an active church. From 'The Normans', it was a short walk to worship at The Chapel of Saint Cross. This did not end with Sunday worship. At every opportunity, any visitor was taken to have their 'wayfarers dole' at the window of The Porters' Lodge, now a little shop, stocking a wide range of high quality items to attract visitors coming to enjoy a tour of the Chapel, its alms-houses, and the beautiful, walled garden. On one occasion, when accompanying a cousin on a tour of Saint Cross, we ended in the Brothers' kithen and dining hall with its ancient artifacts and pump for pumping water into its lead sink. The Brother leading the tour, who was patient in answering David's questions and showing him odd tools, suddenly asked was he a fisherman. The answer came that he had a rod for when he visited Cults, in Scotland, but it was packed away. "Do you know how we catch our fish?" said the Brother. "We just pump and pump and a fish lands in the sink"; surely a joke!

There was a post office on Saint Cross Road alongside the bakery, a general store in Saint Faiths Road, supplying all manner of household goods, including sweets, where a steady stream of children from Saint Faiths school spent their pocket money. Another Post Office occupied a space in Kingsgate Road, opposite The Wykham Arms pub, where Admiral Nelson had once stayed. A post box in the wall marks the position of the Post Office.

The block of flats, in Norman Road, and named 'The Normans', where we took up residence, was quite new and modern for that era in the mid-sixties. Most of the flats were occupied by the owners, who had formed a very active 'association' to determine the needs of residents; gardening, outside repairs, care of communal areas, and general costing. It brought owners together, to discuss these matters quite frequently. Gardening equipment had been purchased, and a committee formed to decide on planting of shrubs and flowers for the square bed laid out in front of our sitting room window. It was a real joy for us to look out on this area, and although I should have liked to take part in its care, my recent injury precluded me from such an activity. Miss Rafferty had occupied her flat from new, and seemed to orchestrate most of the activities at 'The Normans'. She was a lean, sparse lady of definite opinions, but hard-working in her gardening and organising skills. There was a gardening club and its tools, belonging to The Association were kept in what is now the 'bin store'. Needless to say, a rota for grass cutting and general tidying up ensured a bowling green surface, and borders edged. Adjacent to the roadway, another expanse of grass was planted with a few early-flowering ornamental cherries, which are still there, but in poor health. The area is Council owned, but no longer attractive. Grass is cut at quite regular intervals, but clumps of dock leaves now grow in the grass which is cut, but never harvested, leaving the impression of a 'badly-kept field', spreading weeds on to the pavement of Norman Road.

I had attended a sale of work at the Methodist Church in Saint Peter Street [now a complex of flats], and met someone living in the Saint Cross area. We became friends, calling on one another quite regularly, she with her two children struggling from Hubert Road, down the lane to Saint Cross Road and on to number four, The Normans; quite a feat for a little boy of just three. His big sister could take it in her stride, so to speak. Neither could attend Saint Faiths school when the time came, because their parents were not Anglican.

Because of my injured leg, for the first month, David had to entertain himself. I could get along to the swimming pool in Garnier Road, but slowly. He was forced on to his bike which took him far and wide. On one occasion, he had cycled to Sutton Scotney where he met a lady from Colinton, in Edinburgh. She recognised his school blazer and walked along with him, offering to buy him a drink at a little cafe' Back on the main road, he mistook an avenue as a short cut back to Winchester, which led to a mansion house. Meeting a man as he decided to return to the main road, he was invited to sit in the garden and served with lemonade and a cream cake. Apparently, they were not often able to entertain a casual visitor. The mansion, I believe, belonged to J. Arthur Rank, and I was assured that they were very nice.

At this time, a letter arrived from Hampshire County Council Education Department, giving the date and place where boys could sit the eleven plus exam for entry to Peter Symonds Grammar School. This was to take place at the Castle, in Winchester, so off he set on the appointed day. Having been to the Great Hall with his father, he assured me that he knew where to go. Of course, he would see other boys arrive and be able to join the group. Lots of adults were there, he said, and someone in charge asked where his mother was, so he explained about the leg and this person sat with him until the boys were invited into the hall, where desks were set out in rows. The exam was over in no time, and boys could leave when finished. To this day, I have no idea of the content, but I gather it was less stringent than those set as routine at Stewarts College. All that could be done now was wait for a letter from Hampshire Education Department stating the result.

Schools occupied my mind somewhat, with the eleven-plus behind us. Sydney and I had been reluctant to start David's schooling in a class of forty two children, and for that reason had been pleased to pay modest fees to have him in a class of twenty six at Daniel Stewarts.

Things looked very different in Winchester. Prestige in schooling seemed to enter into family life more than in Edinburgh, and certainly more than on Deeside, where pupils stepped down without a thought when learning became a burden, and without a feeling of failure. Of course leaving age was a mere fourteen years, so children grew up quickly and learned some sort of skill to take them through life without a university degree. When going along Kingsgate Road, and admiring the remarkable age of The College buildings, I could not help wondering why so many acres of land and square metres of street housing were necessary to school a few hundred boys at great expense to their families and sacrifice to the community. Was there some sort of prestige to be gained, or just a class thing, which was treated mainly as a joke in Scotland, when taken to this extreme of unnecessary land ownership. It was always a delight to fall upon the scene of boys rowing up or down The Itchen Navigation River.

David did pass his exam for Peter Symonds Grammar School, and in September became a pupil there. Quite a few boys had uniforms handed down from brothers, or other family members. All had long, grey trousers which were not allowed at Stewarts until the age of fourteen, so David appeared in his knee length 'bags' and was asked were they 'short longs or long shorts'.

Our lease of the flat ended at the end of September, and the house at Abbots Ann Road, was complete. Removal of our goods from storage was arranged and our goodbyes said to our neighbours and friends around Saint Cross. Altogether, five families with men working in The Forestry Commission office in Basingstoke would occupy houses in Abbots Ann Road. Four families were Scottish.

There were flaws for the builders to iron out, mainly in the woodblock flooring, which was quite a new concept at this time. A remark was overheard to the flooring group 'get up to that Scots woman about the sanding'. This was a method of getting the blocks perfectly level. But which woman was to be chosen.

The lad made the right guess. Our next door neighbour occupied the house at the end of the cul-de-sac, and we were a small block of four houses, divided from others by a road running off Abbots Ann Road. It gave us the feeling of being quite separate from the remainder of houses on our side of the road. The gardens at back and front sloped downward; in the front, an expanse of grass calling out for a shrub or two, at the back, a bleak prospect. There was an ample driveway, and a garage, but we didn't have a car, which was essential for Sydney to get to work and play his part in the elaborate car-sharing scheme operated by his colleagues travelling to Basingstoke each day.

I was charged with the task of gleaning information about cars, and this was greatly helped by Hyde Abbey Motors, no longer in business. We thought a Ford Anglia would fill the bill, Ford being advised by Alec, Sydney's brother. An Anglia was offered to us, which was a demonstration model, but both of us felt that a new car, just off the blocks would not cost much more. In the end a Cortina was offered, and with discount for payment in cash and in advance, it proved cheaper than the Anglia. Of course, at that time, the car had only a 1.4 engine, with no-power steering, but it was lovely in its coat of near-white paint and smell of newness. I still retain the invoice from its purchase, some five hundred and sixty nine pounds.

It was essential that I could drive the vehicle. We were almost six hundred miles from Aberdeen; too much for one driver, without many rests. My lessons were to cost me no more than twenty pounds, including the test. Mr Harris, of Hyde Abbey Motors would be my tutor. Sydney would accompany me on routes around Winchester and out towards the small villages of Crawley and Sparsholt. Danebury Ring became a favourite destination, going through Stockbridge, up the hill, and into glorious countryside. The avenue towards Danebury presented the ideal area to practice reversing, turning and parking neatly beside some chosen spot. After that, of course, came the delight of walking around the ditches and reflecting on Barry Cunliff's [a local archaeologist] finding about this ancient land mark.

Mr Harris' final route before my test was to Farley Mount from the Romsey Road. I was very confident, bowling along with Nan Trod's Hill of trees on my left, and joining the road to Farley Mount at a sharp bend to the right. That safely accomplished, I entered a road, which was no more than a lane. 'On you go', said Mr Harris, 'and now imagine a lorry coming round the next bend.' I slapped on my brakes and moved to the grass verge, where the jolt came to an end and we both laughed. As with all tests, it depended a little on luck. My reversing was still quite poor and slow. The testing officer was polite, but cold. As we came to Jewry Street, which operated in both directions, a queue of traffic had built up at the side of the street, just opposite The Theatre Royal, and vehicles in front were mounting the pavement to let others pass, coming in the opposite direction. When my turn came to mount the pavement, I was reluctant to forfeit my pass by following the others. The officer made no response to my meaningful looks, so I asked him outright could I follow the traffic without prejudice, and he nodded his head in assent. An emergency stop took place in Garnier Road, without comment, and reverse-parking took place nearby. 'You know, you don't need to take so long to reverse into a marked spot. Really, I thought, expecting this to damn me from a pass. However, on return to the test centre, I was told I had passed and could apply for a driving licence. This was splendid news, not that I wanted to drive around, but I did want to share in the long distances we had to travel. The whole operation came to under budget, and I immediately joined the A.A. from which Association, I received a leather-bound atlas, marking my fifty years membership with it.

Only a single wire fence divided the back garden from our neighbour, and soon after our arrival I spied a little boy watching me from the side of his coal bunker; all houses had open fires and a frequent delivery of coal. He was Christopher and three and a half years old. Although shy at this stage, we were to become great friends as the years progressed. Our coal supplier was a local firm, run by two men. At regular intervals, Mr Goodenough inspected the bunkers of his customers. An order for coal or coke was not necessary because the coalman decided when to fill up the bunker. He opened the lid and if he thought coal was required before his next big round, it would be filled up and a note put through the customer's door. It worked very well.

David, Christopher's elder brother by about eight years, was mildly handicapped and somewhat wilful at times. He became quite obsessed by the coal merchant's lorry, and started taking lifts around Harestock when invited into the cab. A problem arose when he would ask to be let down, often where he could not find his way back home. It was then that, Margaret, his mother, with Sydney helping would search the closes and roads, ringing bells of likely houses of people who knew him. Of course, he was banned from this activity, and the coalman told on no account to take him aboard unless he could be delivered home. It never took place after the time changed and it became dark in late afternoon.

To start with, Scots in Abbots Ann Road stuck together in friendship, and elaborate parties took place at Hogmanay, when we danced, sang and drank toasts. New Years Day in England was not a bank holiday in nineteen sixty six, and its significance was pretty well lost on our English neighbours. It was said that a girl in a long tartan skirt had been seen walking in Abbots Ann Road, with a bottle in her hand at eight thirty in the morning when men were leaving for work. This did not include the revellers, who had taken a day's leave from their office in Basingstoke.

Margaret, being German, celebrated Christmas on Christmas Eve, and by the following year, we shared the celebration with her family, and they with us on New Years eve, before we went out first-footing.

The car share scheme for the men going to the Basingstoke office was working well. Points were allocated for driving and deducted for being a passenger. Sydney's work took him to other parts of the country, quite frequently, so I had sole use of the car a lot of the time. My first journey unsupervised, after taking my test was to visit my Aunt Flora at Frogmore, Windsor. With David navigating, we set off on the A31; there was no M3 or M4, but the volume of traffic was light, compared with present times. Driving gave me a real sense of freedom, that I could reach any part of the country by myself. Petrol was around five shillings a gallon, but not to be wasted.

Once a week Margaret and I shopped together at Sainsbury's, yes exactly where the store is situated to-day. Mac Fisheries was Sainsbury's rival, almost opposite, but facing The High Street. The delivery service from this store was superb; it being difficult to get home before their box of goods arrived at your door. Just like any other county town, Winchester's High Street boasted two large department stores, Dowling's, next to MacFisheries, and Plummers, which had a very nice tea room. The well-known Cadena Restaurant was the hub of eating out at lunch times. It could be difficult to find a table when tourists arrived, in spite of its large area. Waitresses were neatly dressed in black and white, and very attentive, the flaw being that no white linen cloths covered the tabletops.

Interest was attracted to the display of meat in Mr Wright's window farther up The High Street. He was the chosen butcher of most people, supplying Winchester with locally-produced beef, lamb and poultry. There was nearly always a queue at his counter. As a regular customer, I got to know him quite well, and when some time later, he became Margaret's second husband, we already were friends.

Lloyds bank was where I did any financial business. Its huge clock, reaching over the street is to-day still a much admired feature. Should you wish to know if a cheque had been paid, or any other detail, it would be looked up in a ledger and you could be sure the balance was correct, up to the previous night! No series of numbers or complicated telephone calls were necessary to glean information which was bang up to date makes me wonder that we allow ourselves to be corralled into this new method of managing our finances.

The piano had accompanied the rest of our furniture brought from Edinburgh, and now occupied the wall facing the roadway, in the dining room. I knew that a new piano teacher had to be found, but all those recommended seemed bent on their pupils progressing through exams. The wife of the music teacher at Peter Symonds, had pupils, so I asked Mr Perkins if David could become one of her class. This lady was ill and would not be available for a few months. My further search was pre-empted by a call at the door. It was Mr Perkins, bearing a quite battered tenor horn and asking would David like to play this instead, in the meantime. Our association with wind instruments was nil, but David agreed to try it out for the short time of Mrs Perkins incapacity. This resulted in David becoming one of the first boys to join the school brass band which was in the process of being formed. Mr Knight, a Salvation officer and conductor of a Salvation band nurtured the boys into what became 'The Mid Hants Brass Band'. It made for most boys a seven year commitment to performances at home and abroad, and the lifting of many trophies.

In the meantime, a piano teacher still had to be found, and she came in the person of Welsh lady, who mainly gave lessons to mature clients. She was anxious that David sit the progressive exams, but happy to treat him in the same way as her adult pupils, and let him play pieces of his choice and liking. She was no Mrs Geis.

Two children in our road were the source of much amusement and anxiety. They had made friends with the dumper drivers, still working on the site, and got up early to be on site as soon as possible. Big Mick fried his bacon and sausages on his shovel and sometimes burnt his toast if his fire was too fierce. If they were lucky, our small neighbours would receive a piece of toast or a sausage on a plate; sorry another shovel. Rex was brought into their adventures, and he being such an obedient dog answered to all their demands. Large metal pipes lined the end of the cul-de-sac, which was still a through road for these workers. The children somehow managed to get on top of the pipes, cheering and waving as a dumper passed by. Rex, sitting below had orders to bark as they shouted.

It brought neighbours to their doors and windows to make sure it was just the daily ritual of a little boy, a little girl and a dog. The two whispered a lot, making people suspicious of what was to come, and earned them the name of Bonny and Clyde.

Bonny had a huge dolls' pram, usually filled with toy animals, which sometimes included her live, pet hamster. Rex was very alert to when the hamster was brought out, jumping up and down to see what lay inside the pram. It was then that he had to be brought indoors. Should a back door have been left unlocked where the children were mostly welcome, some mischief could await the owner when they returned home. On one occasion the vegetables had been spun in the washing machine. Outside our garden at the back, a deep trench had been dug to extract chalk, the whole area of Harestock being of chalk with little top soil. Inadvertently, a ladder had been left at one end, which attracted the children. They played with a ball in the trench, but when they discovered a pot of white paint thrown into the trench 'she painted me' and 'I painted him' was the call. I surmised that they were covered in chalk when told this, but later their mothers came to tell me that it was indeed paint that had been found, and used, and that they had both been bathed and a lot of Bonny's hair had been cut off.

We arrived home from church one Sunday to find our male neighbours stretched out on the roadway. Learning from the builders, Bonny and Clyde, decided to collect the unset cement from a rain-sodden path and fill in any holes in the road. When they found another small supply, it went into one of the soaka-ways, and now the men were trying to clear it out before it set hard. I was reminded of the children in Edinburgh who followed the craftsmen when our bungalow was being built.

Rex was allowed to wander to a certain extent over the upturned soil before or after a walk, coming to heel a very muddy animal. One day, he did not return, and the children along with me went in search of him, but to no avail. Some time later he approached the house covered in chalk and completely exhausted. We could only guess that he had found his way into a chalk ditch and had struggled to get out.

Laddie, a black Aberdeen Terrier lived across the road from us and was not let out on his own much, but on several occasions, he went astray for a couple of days. Always, it was too late that neighbours had noticed him walk with purpose to the end of the cul-de-sac and out into the world. He did always return safe and sound from his safari.

The Irish Terrier at the end of the street was adept at opening back doors with handles which only needed to be pressed down. It was thought that perhaps the children had helped him acquire this skill. He was found one day curled up and asleep on a neigh-bour's armchair.

The children's piece de resistance came on the opening day of the local pub, The March Hare. Along with a few shops, a butcher, a greengrocer etc. the development was to have its own pub. Word got around that there would be a 'grand' opening on Friday at five thirty. Bonny and Clyde had heard grown-ups making arrangements to attend, and decided they would be amongst the guests. And so, long before the appointed time they were to be seen with pram loaded with toy animals, as usual, crossing the road and entering The March Hare. The staff did not know what to do with the children, who assured them that their parents would be arriving soon. Fortunately, a father from our road had seen them cross to the pub and was able to take them home before their parents became anxious and started a search. At the end of summer, both children were enrolled at the local school. Neighbours and parents expressed sympathy for the teacher who was to cope with this pair. Both children took kindly to being educated, showing an aptitude for books and instruction. They had already demonstrated their ingenuity and curiosity.

Some adults in the street were anxious to be more than friendly with their neighbours. It was after all 'The Swinging Sixties' and large drinks parties were the order of the times. Extra marital sex no longer resulted in a pregnancy, if the woman was on 'The Pill'. Sydney and I were aware of these parties, and had a good excuse ready for our refusal, when the odd invitation came our way. We were marginally older than the average age of twenty five to thirty years, and our regular church going appeared to be a useful barrier to our being invited. Having refused one neighbour twice, we felt our attendance had become obligatory, agreeing to come early and leave to collect David from Youth Club. We enjoyed drinks and conversation with a few neighbours, before numbers beyond the capacity of the house arrived, followed by a group of rugby players calling 'which one to-night?' This was enough for Sydney, as he grabbed my arm and said 'sorry we are leaving, have a nice party'. A voice nearby said 'what's the matter with him then?'.

Short skirts or hot pants were the fashion, the shorter the better, even for those women with ample thighs, squeezed into skimpy outfits. Music blared and shouting and screams reached out from gardens on warm evenings. One evening as Sydney was taking Rex for his evening walk, Lucy, from a house opposite appeared in her night clothes. Thinking some emergency had arisen, he ran after her and when stopped, Lucy just laughed, saying there was no emergency, she was just going to a pyjama party and hoped to see him later on. This raunchy behaviour helped at least four family break-ups to occur in subsequent years.

The Methodist Church in Saint Peter Street was forming 'a wives' group' aimed at occupants of the new housing developments of Harestock and Teg Down. It was to be open to all religions and none. My friend from Hubert Road, in Saint Cross was to become a member. A mix of ages, religions and areas became its formation. This worked well for a time, until remarks like "it's alright for you Catholics, you can just say a few 'Hail Marys' and go and do what you like"'. It did not go down well with many of us. Because most of the group had young children, it was arranged that some talks would be delivered in a members' house. Lady Carpenter-Turner spoke on the subject of being a city magistrate. I presented a case for Mr Powell, who was being vilified in parliament and in the press for his anxiety at the growing numbers of immigrants coming to our shores and having to enter at the foot of our society, where our own poor were struggling to find work and housing. Not many in the group thought him unwelcoming to these people; he wanted it to be better managed with better provision made for their integration into our society at large.

Although I continued attending meetings at Saint Peter Street, most of my friends from Harestock were giving up. In essence, they wanted something nearby, within walking distance, and suggested that I organise something more local. This resulted in the formation of 'The Harestock Young Wives'. We would meet once a fortnight. There would be no constitution, but certain safeguards. Our number would not exceed twelve wives, so that when our husbands were invited to join us we would not be more than twenty four. Wives who enjoyed more raucous parties were not to be welcomed when a vacancy arose. This vetting of a newcomer never became obvious, rather just an observation of how they would fit into our group.

During the first few years of our formation, few changes took place, other than adjustment made to the venue when a new baby arrived. It ended in meetings taking place in the home most suitable according to family circumstances.

I continued to attend meetings at The Methodist Church, but Harestock Wives were more dynamic. Everyone seemed to have a talent, and as Christmas approached, the making of decorations took priority over just chatting. Having gathered greenery and made baubles, we shared our efforts. One spectacular piece which had to be copied several times, was an elegant bough of slim branches, painted white and hung with tiny stars made from gold wrapping paper. Presents of modest cost were brought before Christmas to be placed in a sack from which each of us chose a parcel. One member was mother to five children, a big enough challenge for any family, let alone one where two boys were severely handicapped both mentally and physically. The supporting school of Greenacres played a major part in the lives of these boys, as did their neighbours, and in particular, "The Wives," who supported all charities connected with their condition. Sales of work were supported, and much effort was employed, making items which would sell at these sales. One of the boys had a keen sense of humour, but also a penchant for sticking out his leg with the calliper on it so that his target would stumble. We had to become adept at keeping a safe distance from the offending leg, and sensing when it would be thrust out.

Husbands were to be harnessed twice a year to family duties for the day and evening. Their wives were to have a full day in London, leaving just after breakfast and returning late in the evening. Long lists of duties were left and children instructed on how to look after 'Daddy'. A coach was hired from a local firm, and with trepidation on the first occasion, we waved good bye to our husbands. These visits to London became a great success, even looked forward to by the husbands, left behind in charge of the household.

Parking in London was fairly easy in those days, and we were able to say where we would like to be let down and picked up for the return journey. Our friendly, local coach driver made arrangements for where he could pick us all up for the return journey to

Winchester. At this stage, we split up into small groups, according to the places we wanted to visit. Two of us were able to find seats for 'Miss Saigon', a new musical which was sweeping the West End, featuring the American soldiers' time in Vietnam.

Nearing mid-night, and with a certain anxiety on this first day away, we reached home to be given a relay of events by our husbands, who had coped magnificently with their task of looking after the children.

As a reward for our day of freedom, we took turns in hosting a party to which the husbands were to be present. It followed a pattern of silly games, amazing food and drinks, and some sort of guessing games. Most fun came from the dressing up, when we formed two lines and took turns in donning the clothes taken from a big box and running round to the end of the line. Prizes were awarded to the team finished first. Houses with a dining area as part of the sitting room were best for this contest, since you could enter the kitchen, pass by the staircase into the hallway and join the end of the line. Usually, children of the house would be sitting on the staircase, and although not allowed to join in, were allowed to watch until bedtime. They cheered the strange assortment of characters passing by, in particular men wearing an old pair of corsets round their waist, topped by a smart hat. One man, spying the hearth rug was an animal skin, a tiger, perhaps, gathered it on to his back and bounded past the laughing children on the stairs. They came to regard their parents and others as great fun, cementing friendship between young and old.

Another highlight came in the form of an annual treasure hunt. David and I staked out a route along the lanes of Hampshire with clues to pinpoint certain questions on the sheets of paper given to each car of contestants. This was taken very seriously every time, ending in one man taking his belt from his waist to measure the height of a trig stone to the accuracy of the last centimetre. A mistake occurred when David and I fell upon a field of pig shelters, on the way to Sparsholt. We tried to cover the route as near to the Saturday of the treasure hunt, but on this occasion a quarter of the triangular shelters had been removed by the time of our car rally. Friends got out of their cars to check numbers, but a few shelters had been moved to a place under some trees. The dispute about these shelters raged for years, even in correspondence from Australia, where one family had now settled. The climax of the treasure hunt came with a fish and chip supper at The March Hare, when winners were declared and prizes of chocolate or plants were awarded. My efforts at 'thanks for coming', was met with 'sit down you're drunk', but accompanied by a bunch of flowers from the husbands.

Seven

Two Australian ladies were to join the group on a temporary basis. Their husbands were doctors at The Royal Hampshire County Hospital, and all were keen participants in our activities. That made two doctors, a physiotherapist, four who were Australian, a New Zealander, and three Scots. The remainder from the twenty tour were English. Good friendships were made within the group, resulting in one family staying at our house for a week, before their short tour of the continent and return to Melbourne. Shortly afterwards, a family at the entrance to Abbots Ann Road, decided to emigrate to Australia, and were welcomed by our Australian friends to occupy their garden house while securing a home for themselves in their new country.

For several reasons the country did not engage with them, and after a few years they were back, living near Winchester, and again part of 'The Harestock Wives'.

A feeling of constraint was being felt throughout society; old norms of correct behaviour were being questioned. In schools, children were encouraged to use their imagination, [a good thing] but not at the sacrifice of good grammar and spelling. This took me to the teacher of English at Peter Symonds, to ask that such corrections be made to the boys' work, since David's school in Edinburgh had made spelling so much fun for even younger boys. Books then came back with remarks about 'full stops' and 'paragraphs', which in no way detracted from the content of the work.

Band practice began to play a prominent part in school life. This took place mainly at lunch time, when boys, who would otherwise go home for lunch by bicycle, could sign up for a lunch at school. These were well organized and well disciplined occasions. A top table was set out for sixth formers, and tables for others in front. Boys chose a boy to serve from the meat and vegetable dishes placed on the table. When it was fish, David scored, because some boys were not keen to have a second helping, and because he liked fish, he was expected 'to clean up'. Boys were not allowed to leave school grounds at lunch time until they became sixth formers, when they were allowed to wear a suit, rather than school blazer and grey flannel trousers. The school had a boarding house, where pupils from the Falkland Islands were housed and welcomed by everyone connected with Peter Symonds. No thought emerged that some years later, forces would be sent to these far-off islands to defend their independence from Argentina's aggression.

One feature of the school was that it lacked provision for rugby. There was a hockey team, but not a very active one. Sydney was still keen to play, so both he and David joined a Winchester Hockey club. The brass band was expanding and entering competitions in Winchester Guildhall and in The Albert Hall, London, where it was successful. It now became 'The Mid Hants Band'. To my shame, I did miss one important concert by the band. The Hallé orchestra was performing in Winchester Cathedral, and I succumbed to the opportunity of attending. 'Fingal's Cave' was part of the repertoire, which I did not want to miss. During the interval, when doors were opened in The Cathedral, I could hear sounds of the band coming from the Guildhall. The band was taken to perform on the continent on at least two occasions, once to Germany and once to Permerand in Holland. The boys lodged with interested families, and joined their continental players as marching bands. Mr Knight guarded his boys with an eagle eye, making their welfare his top priority at all times. At the end of the Dutch tour, I received a letter from David's hosts saying how much they had enjoyed his company, and the meal he had cooked of herring coated in oatmeal. Soon after the band's return, Sydney received a parcel by post, containing a box of cigars. It was a gift from David. Older boys had been able to buy cigarettes, but because of his age, David could not bring this through 'customs' and decided to use the postal system.

At one of our meetings at The Methodist Church, my friend from Hubert Road, suggested that I join her and her husband at a dance club being held in Alresford. I jumped at the opportunity, and she added 'would Sydney like to come as well?'. In spite of his love of ballroom dancing, I did not think he would relish an evening spent Scottish Country dancing. She wondered if I would mind asking him. Of course, I had no objection and not much expectation that the answer would come back 'yes'. His reply in the affirmative sealed over forty years of our dancing together in this fashion.

Each week, we congregated in a school hall in Sun Lane, Alresford to be instructed in reels and strathspeys by a very sporty lady. Miss Greenfield was headmistress of Greenacres School for handicapped children, just off the Andover Road in Winchester. There were five Scots, and we were outnumbered two to one by the English. Sydney was the only one with a kilt.

As we progressed, a Burns Supper was held in The Beauworth Village hall, arranged by one of the farmers in the group. I could not understand why Sydney was writing a long explanation of the life of Rabbie Burns, but it was well received by the company, not all dancers, who knew little of this national poet. Sydney, who had learned to recite 'Tam O'Shanter' at school delivered this poem to a most appreciative audience, in what was a most suitable setting. After two years together, we were sent out to fend for ourselves in clubs around Winchester, where members were expected to find instructions for dances from the many books published, and be able to execute all figures and footwork necessary. It was something of a challenge to start with, but soon mastered. Some of us joined The Waverley Scottish Dance Club, which at that time functioned in Saint Paul's church hall, near Winchester railway station. It attracted about fifty dancers, and was run by Jock Souter, a prison officer who brought along three girls from the prison service. It now was a case of being truly hooked on this pastime.

Invitation dances were held in the halls of larger schools, attracting dancers from Southsea, Southampton and farther afield. Tickets were restricted to eighty people, with many disappointed, since an elaborate buffet was provided at the break. One memorable occasion was when our annual ball was held in The Guildhall, Winchester, where near to three hundred assembled for dancing to a band brought down from Scotland to play for us. It was quite a sight to see the men, all in kilts, with their partners in pale evening dresses with a tartan sash pinned to their right shoulder. Catering for such a company had to be left for the Guildhall staff, but a bar was open for drinks; a poor return for the Guildhall, since water was mostly drunk by the perspiring company.

Waverly Club was moved to Holy Trinity church hall, North Walls, which was bigger in area, and near to the central car park, recently laid out. Numbers increased, so it was easy to attract enough people when a big dance was proposed. Demonstrations were sought in the city and performed at the Butter Cross, where traffic could just squeeze past. The Art College presented some demonstrations, before the new recreation building with swimming pool was completed.

The 'Young Wives' had spent the winter making craft items for the coming sales of work. It was time to enjoy the outdoors. Local maps were scoured for likely footpaths around Winchester. When these routes had been walked, cars were taken to Farley Mount, so that part of The Clarindon way could be walked. This skirted Stockbridge, and afforded interesting views of the surrounding countryside. Should only ten walkers be present, two cars were taken to opposite ends of the route chosen, so that we could pass in the middle. It came as a relief, when we spied the group approaching from their other starting point. Since two members had identical models of cars, they were able to complete the walk and drive the other's car home. Only once was a Cortina driven into the wrong driveway on return, without a thought that it didn't belong there.

Parties were given a new concept. Three small groups were formed to give a small performance to the husbands and the other members. It was started with a ditty sang by all members to the tune 'A Darkies' Sunday School', an American tune well known then, but banned no doubt nowadays. It went;

"Harestock Wives are very versatile, with songs and poems and merry quips, your time we will beguile'.

Leave your washing, leave your knitting, leave your husbands baby-sitting.

Join our happy company and have yourselves some fun."

Two members, who were tall and slim wore hot pants, a fashion of the sixties, the rest of us wore colourful skirts and tops. All wore appropriate hats. The skits which followed were hilarious, and bordering on the vulgar at times, particularly those conceived by the nurse and physiotherapist, using treatments unknown to man.

Neighbours got wind of our gatherings, and wondered what we did that brought so much jollity and good will, but the secret was never divulged.

With yet another garden brought to heel, I had to find some

voluntary work. This came as help in the geriatric ward of Saint Pauls Hospital, now a block of flats near Saint Pauls church and the railway station. I signed up for two days a week, Mondays and Fridays, and was issued with a white coat and badge.

The intake was of elderly and infirm ladies from the Winchester area. It was run on hospital lines, ten ladies making up the ward and all in open view, with screens when personal attention was required. An ex-naval sister was in charge, with a staff nurse helping her. Sister was kind, but forthright with her patients, as the ladies were termed. I chose to arrive at nine thirty each duty day, and could find a queue of ladies waiting to be bathed. This I could help to do with a junior nurse in charge. A hoist was seldom required, but I was shown how to operate it.

Feeding some ladies was necessary, and a peculiar phenomenon came to light in that food was saved in the lockers of some people. Perhaps, it was something not liked, or the fear that another meal would not appear. Cleaning out of lockers became a worthy act. Staff were reluctant to interfere with ladies personal effects, and had little time to answer long-overdue letters, or admire photographs of family and friends. One lady who had lived in Saint Thomas Street thought I brought her cat with me. She could 'see it at the window' which gave her great pleasure and me many thanks. Another lady could only return to her home when her grandson was on night shift, when she could sleep in his bed. She was very fit, but obviously suffered from some form of dementia. It was she who asked me to make her a cold water sandwich. In spite of many operations, taking place over her ninety seven years of life, she was fitter than her daughter of eighty, who struggled each week to climb the stairs, receiving no appreciation of the effort.

Occasionally, an appointment was made for a lady to attend the main hospital, and who required someone to accompany her. This could take away a nurse from her duties for a long spell. I was useful in this area. The ambulance team was always cheerful, even when describing some gruesome event which they had just attended; cutting down a man who had hanged himself!

Some ladies were still able to go shopping if accompanied, and it fell to me to take two ladies to Dowlings, a store next to MacFisheries on the High Street, one to be fitted for new corsets and the other for new shoes.

Two dark-skinned nurses joined the ward, far from home, one from America, the other from The Caribbean. They appreciated being invited for tea, and together we pushed Muriel in her invalid chair all the way to Abbots Ann Road. Muriel was a young person, misplaced in a geriatric ward, but soon to be moved to more suitable care.

Both nurses were anxious to spread their wings, one to London, and one to New York, where she thought her experience here would advance her promotion. Both obtained their aims, but not before we had heard some brilliant play on our piano from the Caribbean girl. So engrossed was she while playing, that she flew off the end of the stool. Fortunately, she was not hurt.

Within a couple of months, all three had left Saint Pauls, Muriel, the young lady in the wheelchair, who had suffered a stroke, to a unit with people nearer to her age group, the others to America and the Caribbean.

Although far from the immediate families, we did not lack visits. In nineteen sixty seven, I was able to show my parents around Saint Cross, and take their photograph crossing over the field towards the Clarindon Way. Most of the equipment in the Brothers kitchen was familiar to my mother and intriguing to all of us. The Brother again told us that fish were at one time brought from the tank in The Master's garden by pump. We never did check on this statement.

Both my youngest sisters visited; Marion for a whole summer, when she was employed at Saint Pauls, before setting out to be a teacher and moving from Glasgow to The Bahamas and America. At this time, the hospital was run by a matron, who visited her wards each morning, pointing out any slackness in cleaning or orderliness, all wheels carrying beds had to face away from the door and sluices polished. An 'extra work book' sat on sister's desk with tasks for the day listed, e.g. cleaning behind beds, and dusting down walls, to be done by anyone with a spare moment and signed. Marion kept me well informed as to what would be a priority when I arrived after her on one of my mornings.

Christmas was the time when we met the families of our charges. The ward had become very festive and we looked forward to visits from The Mayor and The Rotary Club. We had a Mayoress, and volunteers were invited to parade behind the entourage and shake hands with each lady. Gifts were shared amongst the staff, but volunteers each received a generous gift from The Rotarians. Some nurses found it difficult to get to work on Christmas Day, and since our 'Special Day' was New Years Day, and we had celebrated Christmas with our neighbours the evening before, I was able to substitute for a nurse whose journey would have been difficult. Preparations for our Christmas meal was safely left in the hands of Sydney and David.

By nineteen seventy four, laws had changed drastically, for the management and administration of our hospital. Cleaners were brought in from agencies, hospital funding was changed, and Basingstoke became "head" office for the Winchester area. An administrator came from Basingstoke each week to examine work done in the small offices left in each hospital. I was called to visit the office by a man from Basingstoke, who enquired why I turned up at nine thirty and worked only two days a week. He was quite speechless, when I told him I was only a volunteer and that many tasks would not be done for the ladies, if we did not come. I took this opportunity to ask what tasks I was not allowed to perform, and received the answer that I could not give out medicines. In fact apart from this one task, my work was the same as that of the nurses.

This turn around of administration did not resonate with our previous, sensible approach, and most of us left. The "extra work" book was discarded, and ticking of boxes introduced. Cleaners were to be called in for minor clean-up jobs, at added expense to the system. Only staff were to help ladies to their sitting room, which became little used.

The headmistress of Greenacres School, just off the Andover Road, and who had established the dance club at Alresford needed help in running a club for her older handicapped pupils after school. This resulted in my transfer of two days a week from Saint Pauls to Greenacres School. The atmosphere was active. Swimming and outdoors activities were encouraged. The headmistress taught her pupils to swim on her own back, and drove the mini-bus on most outings. She made no concessions to struggles where they could be overcome, and be of benefit to the pupil. Music played a big part with an assembly each morning, when one hymn was sung, the favourite being "Sing Hosanna" and sung with great gusto.

Although the headmistress held her post as an educationalist, her staff were previously employed as social nurses, and not teachers. Now they were to be given the status of teacher, so well deserved, since that was what they were delivering.

I was allocated to help and learn from such a lady. Her wisdom and imagination in getting the best out of her, sometimes unruly class, gained my admiration, and the hope that I could emulate this. My main charge was a girl from Romsey who suffered epileptic fits, brought on spontaneously and which could be oftener than three times a day. With me in attendance, classwork could continue without disruption.

Through the odd concert for parents, and others interested, talents for singing and playing instruments were exposed and appreciated. One girl who was part of a nomad camp, gave her act as the birth of a baby. She writhed on the floor screaming and panting and produced a doll at the end. She was obviously re-enacting something that she had seen, and was quite sulky at being told she would be better playing her drum at the concert.

Greenacres had a splendid cook, and my perk was that I could look forward to delicious lunch on the days I was there.

Visits to the newly opened Lido swimming pool, adjacent to the cattle market on the Andover Road, became very crowded in summer, mainly by French scholars come to Winchester to improve their English, and boarded by local families. David and some of his school friends changed their activity of swimming to fishing. The council issued permits to young people to fish the stretch between the City Mill and Wharf Mill at a modest cost. This stretch was not without trout, but a better result came by letting the rod dangle behind you in the Itchen, beyond the Wharf Mill. Towards evening, the rivers teemed with fish, leaping to catch caddis flies, and other insects skimming the surface of the water.

My ambition to catch sight of a kingfisher was not realised until many years ahead, in spite of my arrival at sites where one had been spotted, particularly in The New Forest.

By the age of fourteen, boys were finding part-time jobs to earn some pocket money. David was to caddie on Hockley golf course for a surgeon from the hospital and his lawyer companions. This led to friendship between old and young, as on Harestock, with 'The Wives' Group' and their families. A visit was made by David to the surgeon's holiday house just outside Ballater, while Sydney and I were visiting Braemar.

Sydney's and my golf clubs were packed into the boot of the car, when two boys joined David for a round at Southampton Municipal Course. I was required to drive them there and back, and of course participated in the round. A friendly foursome of men behind us very kindly pointed out the ladies 'tee' some thirty yards nearer the flag, and on level ground, but I always teed off with the boys, so a chorus gave the answer, "She can hit the green from here". I hit the ball with full force, and because the weather had been dry, the ball ran well, just touching the edge of the green, at the finish. The remark from behind was "she is just little, she must be Scotch."

The boys were working hard for their "O" levels, most taking ten, David twelve. There seemed to be little anxiety about results, and little competitiveness as to who did better than anyone else. Founder's Day came and went, David stamping on his buttonhole of Sweet William as soon as the Cathedral service was over: Sweet William being named for Butcher Cumberland, persecutor of the Scots. One boy, who had just passed his driving test, found the ideal job. He had to drive his employer to the railway station from just short of Stockbridge and fetch him home about five thirty in the afternoon. All the amenities of the manor house were at his disposal while he carried out a bit of gardening or tidying up. The staff were instructed to provide his mid-day meal. Time hung heavy, in spite of there being a swimming pool, so if the weather was fine, David and I were collected on his way back from the station to spend the day by the swimming pool.

David's application to become cleaner for Hiltingbury School, during the summer, was successful, but the work ended after a week, when the authorities discovered he was not eighteen. Soon however, having passed his driving test straight after his seventeenth birthday, he obtained work, driving a van for a local bakery. This took him out into the countryside, mostly towards Alresford, calling on Police houses at Itchen Abbas, and driving a mile up a lane at Privet, where the lady's door was left open for him to supply the order left with money on the kitchen table, if she had gone out. Always there was fruit or vegetables for him to take away.

Four of his close friends applied for entry to Oxford University. The other boy was bent on London School of Economics. I drove David to Worster College, Oxford for a two part interview, and we were graciously received and shown around the college.

We were introduced to a student who would be living on the same floor, should an offer be made. It had come as a surprise to Sydney and myself, when David announced that he wanted to change his mind about studying chemistry, and study mathematics instead. Apparently, he was very fond of his chemistry master and enjoyed his lessons, but only the mathematics part of the subject interested him. The school was very good about the change, but pointing out "you choose Oxford above everywhere else", a concept not in tune with either Sydney's or my sentiments. Oxford gave him the opportunity to apply to study mathematics there, but more than expected had been cut from the school curriculum to gain an offer at such short notice. The University of Durham, after some catch-up time, offered a more acceptable course, and it was there that he found himself, shortly after his eighteenth birthday, with our discarded car.

Time was running out for our sojourn in Winchester. Rumours abounded that The Forestry Commission's headquarters in Basingstoke was not prestigious enough, and that it might occupy a new building, under construction in Edinburgh. This turned out to be the case and, although Civil Servants were offered transfers to The Civil Service Commission, now situated in Basingstoke, Sydney and I felt that we owed it to Scotland to return there. Having seen the serried ranks of staff set out in order of rank, at one of the C.S.C.'s functions, we would not have felt comfortable there after our gregarious meetings at 'Porters', a sometime venue for our gatherings, where officers and guests shed their ranks in the interests of enjoying the gathering.

The day came when an announcement was made officially to staff that Forestry Commission headquarters would move to Edinburgh. Sydney's department would be first to move; in fact his move did not take place for a year.

David was in Durham, but my young next door neighbour, Christopher, was always at the ready to accompany me on a round of golf, a long walk, or as a passenger to collect Sydney from Heathrow, on his return from Scotland or the west of England. It felt strange being in limbo once again. A return to Edinburgh was welcomed in many respects, but our roots went deep in Hampshire. We had made life-long friends here and our activities were flourishing.

I told my headmistress at Greenacres that my time was limited, and she countered with the proposal that I accept the vacancy which had occurred for the care of my charge from Romsey, who was being offered hours of attention, paid for by the Education Department. This commitment would be short term and temporary, but every day of school attendance. I needed time to think this out with regard to our future move. I decided; no more gardening, not so much golf and visitors left to their own devices, when school called.

Pay was a pittance, and swallowed up in tax when added to my husband's salary. I received a pension from Hampshire County Council of the amount of two postage stamps for the eleven months, in spite of my requests that it be stopped.

This is looked back on as a most enjoyable time with staff and pupils, but without the large donation I expected to make from working.

Rex did not survive to participate in our removal to Edinburgh. He died from a growth at the side of his head caused by, the vet said, 'eating too much tinned food'. David supported me in taking Rex to be put down. "Mother is it really necessary to go down the Stockbridge Road at quite such speed?". My anxiety to have the deed over and done with, had taken up my thoughts and actions.

Several months after Rex had died, an advertisement appeared in the local newspaper with chow chow puppies for sale. Since my encounter in childhood with Chang in Cults, it had been my desire to own a dog of this breed, with its immense coat of soft hair and blue tongue. The three of us hastened to Havant, where the puppies were to be seen, and one hopefully chosen. Three were male and one a bitch. They ran around their garden, in and out of bushes, like big balls of wool. One kept coming back to David, but it was the bitch, and Sydney was not keen. However she became the choice and came home with us, after assurances that all inoculations would be given. How does one find a name for a Chinese dog, was the question. This was solved almost immediately, when we had a speaker at church, who had spent many years in Shanghai, and now lived in Hampton Lane, Winchester. Her suggestion was Mai lei Ming; Beautiful Brightness. No dog could have been so misnamed. Beautiful, she certainly was, but bright as in intelligent - no. Our efforts to teach her even the rudiments of safety or habit fell on deaf ears. Her response was to lie down. This led to people asking did we love Ming as much as we had loved Rex. In a strange way, we all did, but a comparison was impossible. She was protective of us, the house and the car in her laid-back way.

Children loved her mass of hair, and the girl opposite used to call most days to take Ming for a walk round the block before school. She was too languid to wander off, often sitting on the driveway opposite our house. It seemed a strange thing to be doing, until we realised she was guarding the baby in his pram, with a growl to the postman as he passed her.

Our families were pleased by the prospect of our return to Scotland. My parents and Sydney's sister and brothers, had all spent time with us in Winchester, even working here in the case of my sister, Marion. Sydney's niece had come with her family of boys in their ancient Ford car from just outside Glasgow to enjoy The New Forest, considered by them as just a big park, compared with the vast forests of Norway spruce in the west of Scotland. There were picnics, games of rounders and interesting walks and, of course, the ponies.

At the foot of our garden, a row of sheltered bungalows had been built, and several of us had made good friendships with the occupants, most of whom were widows. One, in particular was of great interest to me. She was Lebanese, married to an ex British Army officer. She kept up with all aspects of life in Egypt and the Middle East. Her religion was Christian, and she was very afraid of the turmoil engulfing the area at that time. Her command of English was remarkable, but described in this way – 'My English is broke'. Many happy hours were spent in my kitchen, following instructions of how to make a Middle-eastern pudding of exotic fruits, or a cake with dates. A lot of dates were used, and a lot of cabbage, as a vegetable, maybe a substitute for a plant not grown in this country. One day, I was given a pile of Egyptian coins with an engraving of the Sphynx on each, and dated nineteen hundred. Later on, when I had attended a class on silver smithing, I was able to use pure silver to join them together into a unique bracelet.

On our penultimate visit to Deeside prior to leaving Winchester, it was arranged so that we would bypass Aberdeen, making our way via Perth to Braemar, where we would stay at the Invercauld Arms Hotel. Our object was that we would walk from Lynn of Dee to Aviemore, that was David and me. Sydney was to pick us up by car at the end of our trek through The Larig Ghru, an ancient drove road between Deeside and Speyside.

The weather was fine as we filled our lungs with mountain air. In no time, we had traversed Glen Dee, that sad glen, with its piles of overgrown stones which had once been homes. At the white bridge, we crossed to have a better view of Cairn Toul on our left, and the outcrop of The Devil's Point. On crossing back, I had to be dragged out of the water by my son, both of us laughing. Our next stop was opposite Corrour Bothy, a wooden sanctuary for travellers in fog or storms. It was a joy to linger by the pools of Dee where this turbulent river begins its course to the sea at Aberdeen. The path was now all boulders, but fairly distinct in its direction, as we plodded on towards the heather.

All of a sudden, I found myself on hands and knees on the sloping bank of grass and heather. 'What are you trying to do?', I shouted, 'You were about to step on an adder', came the answer. I was the one supposed to know these hills, and I had missed something I had been warned from early years to look out for.

One big sign I did not miss, came from the weather. As the footpath rose, I began to feel uneasy. Sun had shone intermittently. We were now high up on the track between Brae Riach and Ben MacDui when I became aware of soft puffs of air coming towards us. The hair on the back of my head, I am sure reacted." We have to hurry along now and get down from this place." The warning came from my innate sense of danger from fog, which would soon engulf us on this dangerous part of the path, so narrow and a steep fall to a burn on our right. Ptarmagan, on the slope were gently feeding on a grassy mound, still in the their summer outfits. It is well that we hastened through this part of The Larig Ghru, because my instinct of fog was soon proved true.

Having reached lower ground, and with a view of Loch Morlich on our right, but still far off, and Rothiemurchas Forest in front of us, a decision had to be made as to which route to follow. As we stood there, leaning towards taking the route to Loch Morlich far to our right and in a hollow bathed in sunshine, a figure emerged from the trees far below us. It was Sydney, and only the second person we had met during our hike; such a coincidence that he should appear at that precise moment just before we had taken our decision. He had seen mist descend to cover the summit of Cairngorm and decided to enter the Larig Ghru to see if we had made it through to lower ground.

Continuing through the silent forest, there was time to contemplate the journeys along this ancient drove road, where in olden times, cattle were driven towards Braemar and onward to the cattle markets farther south. There were few grazing patches at this level, but farther south in Glen Shee for example, large areas of grassland can be seen where stops could be made, always beside a loch or burn for cattle to graze and drink.

Our three day stay at Aviemore, meant trekking each day.

Loch Morlich was busy with little boats, and children paddling. We climbed Ben Avon and Cairngorm, where on a previous visit, we had seen lads skiing in swimming trunks in May. The weather had been hot, but the snow runs were still snow-bound. An indication of the winter activity stood in the hallway of the hotel, a miniature set of skis. They belonged to Morag aged eight and she was getting on fine at the skiing.

Upon arrival at my parent's house in Cults, I met with my cousin Billy, of few words, who was visiting. No greetings were exchanged, only a dig in the ribs, and 'I hear you've been through the Larig Ghru', said in his usual gruff voice. He had all the Munroes under his belt and had climbed near to the top of Mont Blanc. [A Munroe is a mountain over three thousand feet in height]. Most in this country are in Scotland.

At the age of sixty five, my father retired and was offered the option of staying in 'Fairview' by the river, or having a new council house in West Cults, near to a bus service and a short walk to Cults West Church. He opted for the latter, feeling that the steep brae to Cults and its amenities might become too strenuous in later years. Still fit, in spite of his stomach problem, a friend from the Post Office at Bieldside offered him a cycling job for fun. This entailed delivery of mail to out-lying farms and country houses, including that of Lady Fermoy, Princess Diana's grandmother. This work took up only part of the day and was a cycle run of about twelve miles. At Christmas, tips were more than generous, and during the round, old friends were met and news exchanged. Sadly this came to a sudden halt, when my father suffered a stroke and fell downstairs. The news came to me the day of the accident, but being still in Winchester, I was unable to get to Aberdeen in time to see him before he died. His birthday was on Saint Andrew's day, and for years, I could not bring myself to dance on that night.

By nineteen seventy, all my sisters were living away from Cults: Flora, married and living in Huntly, Christine, who had been married for a short time to a scientist, who was to follow a Maharishi to India. She was now nursing in Portsmouth, and Marion, teaching in Freeport, Bahamas. We were a far-flung family. Flora was soon bringing up three children in Aberdeenshire. Kevan had left the care of his grandparents, and had a new brother and a new sister. They were twins. Flora's new husband was slightly cripple from an attack of Polio, just after the war. He was in business as a Car instructor, and doing some maintenance work on cars. Flora received a severe shock when her husband died from a stroke when the twins were but two years old. Flora, always good with figures, managed to salvage some of the business, and carried on without complaint. Some years later she married a local man, also with a business. His clients, mostly farmers took advantage of his good nature, paying with bags of tatties [potatoes] or a piece of beef. Flora quickly put an end to this by making out bills, and telephoning the wives and explaining to the unsuspecting women that she required cash. Mostly, they were shocked and payment was made in cash or by cheque in future.

Christine's situation was complex. While other mothers were trying to keep boyfriends out of their daughters bedroom, Mother was trying to bring her newly weds into a normal, married relationship. It did not work. There would have to be a divorce, which in those far-off days, could not be granted within two years. Few people in Cults knew of this trauma. Christine had been nursing in Glasgow for some time, dealing with the 'razor gangs' of the time. She described the injury section on a Saturday night as a blood bath. In one night there had been no fewer than twenty four knifings. This behaviour was stopped to a great extent, when sentences of sixteen years in prison were handed out to the perpetrators. However, these youths would never attack a nurse or elderly woman. Their code of conduct did not allow this, no man could hurt a Granny! Christine accepted a post in The General Hospital in Portsmouth. It was severely understaffed, particularly at night, when only one person would be on duty for the whole ward. Only the ringing of a bell could summon help. An advertisement requiring nursing staff for a big Copper Company, in Zambia, attracted an application from Christine and she was successful. The uniform allowance was almost the equivalent of her present salary. Mufulira in the copper belt of Zambia, was her destination.

She grew to love and admire the native population, and enjoyed the wild life of the lately established nature reserves. Youths here would snatch a purse or handbag from anyone. Unlike in Glasgow, nurses were not exempt. This tiny nurse chased a thief down an alley, followed by her friends, fearing that she would be injured. Upon turning a corner, they saw Christine shaking her finger at a big fellow, purse in hand and fumbling to give him a few coins. 'They have so little.' she said.

Marion, too, had worked in Glasgow. After teaching in an affluent school in the western part of Aberdeen, she and a colleague decided to teach in a really poverty Stricken area of Glasgow. A huge scheme of slum-clearance had taken place in the city, and vast housing estates, like Easterhouse, had been built.

Class numbers were over forty, but children were obedient, and willing to learn. Progress was less than expected during the first year, but Marion had the same class the following year which was their last before secondary school. This time they were familiar with the routine of the class, its rules, and punishments.

Parents were welcomed at special evenings, and directed towards libraries, where appropriate. Boys were encouraged in sport, and girls taught to knit [for when they have their babies, in a few years time!]. Kath, Marion's colleague, had married a doctor from Austria, who wanted to return there, so she was now in Vienna.

By chance, on a bus, one cold winter's day, Marion noticed two advertisements for teachers, one for Canada, and the other for The Bahamas. She applied for both, and had given up hope of a reply from either, when a response came from the one for The

Bahamas, inviting her to attend an interview. Her interviewer had been educated at Robert Gordons School in Aberdeen, with a sister known to Marion from her school days at The Girls' High. This man knew the rigors of Marion's training, and educational standing, so the interview rested on reminiscing on Aberdeen, and what to expect at Saint Paul's, Freeport. This put an end to Canada as a contender, although snow skiing, a much-loved sport would not be possible in the tropics. A replacement was soon to be found in water skiing, her instructor telling me that he had never known anyone to get up on their skis as quickly as Marion.

In a macabre way, Billy, Fora's cripple husband had insured Flora's life for a large sum of money, thinking that should some accident occur, and that he was unable to care for Kevan and the twins, money would not be a problem. Flora did not view this a sensible move.

Kevan, now almost a teenager, was Flora's rock. The twins, boy and girl, both with red hair, were bundles of mischief, helping one another into grotesque situations. Flora had continued parts of the business, she could manage, which meant the doorbell rang frequently. Grabbing a twin under each arm, and exclaiming 'Oh me, me' she would answer the call. Going along the street, one day there was a lot of pointing at doorways and saying 'me, me', the children thought the name for a doorbell was 'me, me'.

To keep some sort of memory of their father, the twins were taken to the graveyard to see his grave, and play there; not approved of by a couple of elderly widows, but cheered by Billy's friends, who knew him to have a keen sense of humour.

In Zambia, Christine had met a young professional in the employ of Rio Tinto Zinc, whose home was in Southampton. He was keen to have Christine as his bride, but she had some time to go in her application for divorce from her marriage, which had been in name only. Upon return to Britain, Christine found herself with a huge tax bill if she returned to paid employment before the end of the tax year, in March. She decided to throw in her lot on a voluntary basis with Rudolf Steiner Village, not far from her home in Cults. She and Barry were married when he returned to this country, and soon had two little girls.

As a family, they returned to Africa, this time to Botswana, before that country had found its plethora of mineral wealth. There was some anxiety about inoculations for children so young, but all was deemed safe. A land rover was purchased to take goods from Southampton docks. It could be sold for a profit when it reached its destination of Selebi-Pikwe. The family sailed on the same ship.

The ship docked in Cape Town, and the long hazardous drive to their new home began. They passed many small villages with round, thatched roofs. Clothes were bright and colourful when local people appeared. One man was proud of his leather shoes, one black and one brown, and slightly different in size. Why should shoes be the same for each foot?

Upon arrival, it became clear, that one was expected to hire help in the garden and house, in all aspects of living. The local economy depended on it. A young lady arrived to help with the unpacking. She admired a piece of material, red and yellow, which covered some shelves in the kitchen. She was offered it to take away, as surplus, and next day appeared at the gate resplendent in a gown made from the material, with matching headgear.

Sydney and I were able to meet them on their return by liner to Southampton, the girls now three and a half and two years old. The onward journey was to Aberdeen and on to The Rudolf Steiner Village, near Cults, of which they were to become part. This would be a very rural life for my nieces, with animals, poultry of all description, to be looked after and fed. The ride to nursery school was by pony and trap, along the defunct Deeside Railway route. It was quite a joy to find that the girls did not define anyone by the colour of their skin. When asked at the station who had dropped money, the answer came 'grey man,' a man wearing a grey suit, who was also coloured. It did not seem to register that his skin was his most outstanding feature, amongst the others milling around.

Tragedy struck this family too, when Barry was diagnosed with an aggressive cancer at an early age. He would not live to see his girls grow up into the beautiful persons they were to become.

Eight

MARION WAS WELL SETTLED IN FREEPORT AND SAINT PAULS School. Thespian urges became real in the production of 'Lion in Winter', a Shakespeare play, in which she played a leading role. At this distance, she was not cut off from family. Mother visited from time to time, as did I and David and June with my granddaughter, Elaine. Only Mother was able to attend her marriage in the beautiful Garden of The Groves, a haven for humming birds seeking nectar from the displays of tropical plants.

As well as being an accountant, Marion's husband was a keen aviator, piloting a small plane between Freeport and Nassau, when a visitor wished to visit the Capital. It was exciting to fly at such a low level, and look down on the cruise ships, with passengers relaxing on the decks. We flew over the tiny islands of Bimini and Eleuthera, with their clear patches of cannabis in view.

Nassau held all the delights of a Caribbean capital. Marion used Wells Fargo as her car insurer, and when asked directions to its office a huge ethnic policeman offered to take us. He recognized our Scottish accents and had received his training at Tulliialian, the police training centre, near Edinburgh, so had many questions to ask about the city.

Shopping, for the most part, was carried out in Florida, the journey being made by cruise ship to Fort Lauderdale or Miami. It seemed odd not to be part of the holiday scene, not joining in pool games, skeet shooting, or gambling in casinos. My mother did go to see a show one evening on board one of these ships. It was known to be a bit 'risqué', so in case the minister of the local church in Freeport, felt he had better not view this stuff, she decided to describe its contents and give an opinion; a bit vulgar, but not too bad; 'a second-rate Tivoli show'. The Tivoli, in Aberdeen was less conventional than His Majesty's Theatre, and considered down-market.

The celebrations for our silver wedding in Aberdeen, went ahead and, although it was expected that Marion and her husband would attend, only she was able to make the journey. The occasion was one of fun and pleasure for us, with so many of both families together in The Gloucester Hotel. Another group occupied the other half of the dining room, but it was not long before we integrated, when dancing commenced in the adjoining ballroom.

Marion had indicated that she was returning to Freeport to try to start a family. Sadly, this would never happen. Upon her return, she discovered that her husband was in the middle of an affair with a fellow Canadian woman. The shock must have been devastating. Fortunately, good friends surrounded her. For myself, I wished that I had heeded some pointers, made to me by those friends, that he had a roving eye and that their warning was meant to be passed on. It was not on the scale of tragedy which befell my other two sisters, nevertheless, it brought disruption and divorce.

Apart from our twice annual visits to Aberdeen, we managed to fit in a holiday to Cornwall or North Devon. The wildness of Dartmoor resonated with me, since reading of its ancient forest, and Bronze-age hut circles. The sea dragged us to Newquay, with its golden beach, and roiling waves. The Beechcroft Hotel, where we stayed, sat on the edge of the cliff, with a private footpath leading down to the beach. Some years later, it was to fall off its precarious perch onto the beach below.

Preparations were well afoot for our move to Edinburgh, new houses were being built, just off the Queensferry Road, in Edinburgh. This location suited us well, since a footpath led over Corstorphine Hill, to the zoo entrance, right opposite the entrance to The Forestry Commission's new office.

We had discarded the idea of buying a lovely bungalow on Queensferry Road, with its busy traffic, and another house at Cramond, near the Forth estuary, but directly under the flight path to Turnhouse, Edinburgh's airport. Mr Meikle, from whose firm we would in the end purchase our new home, had a waiting list of over one hundred interested clients. All of us felt despondent, and even encouraged us to consider living outside the city, in Dalkeith, perhaps.

At one of his school reunions, David sat next to someone connected with Mr Meikle, and when told that we wanted to purchase one of the new houses, assured him that the list was mainly for advertisement, and most of the names would disappear. It was not long before a letter arrived to say that subject to mortgage etc.. a house would be reserved for Sydney. Plans were sent to Winchester, and I was able to ask if the one at the end of the row, with larger acreage, could be ours.

Days were racing past. Time was running out. The exploits of The Mid Hants Band, their trips overseas, and the visit of the Finnish family, who stayed with us during their tour with their band, would soon be just memories belonging to Winchester.

Now that a young family from the west country, were to be occupants of our house in Abbots Ann Road, a farewell party had to be arranged. It was to include a variety of ages and people. The boy across the road found 'Southern Music', of Littleton, a band prepared to play some Scottish dance music, keen in fact, because his father was a Scot. Numbers mounted, with friends from school, church, neighbours, and The Young Wives. The hall of the pub, later becoming "Chimneys", just off Stockbridge Road was booked. They did not provide food, but caterers could be brought in, and there were plenty tables and chairs to bring out for the company to sit around.

A big snag hit us the day before the party. Our young family had a sick baby, and their removal packed to be delivered at noon the day after the party. We felt we had no alternative but to let them enter the house as our guests, since enough furniture was being left to make this possible. Margaret, next door was to be in charge and be on hand to help out. The food problem was easily solved by The Wives, who collected my orders from the greengrocer, who refused payment for lettuce, tomatoes, and cucumber. The delicatessen provided a selection of meats and cheeses. Rolls and cake came from the Master Baker, next door.

The staff in the pub were most helpful, providing after eights, with tea and coffee after the meal. We danced modern and Scottish, the father of the bandsman, joining in. It was a most enjoyable farewell, poignant, when we all joined hands to sing Auld Lang Syne.

We were not left on the street at this point, our Scottish friends at Kingsworthy, had offered us hospitality for the night. It was almost a relief to get up early next morning, have breakfast, and be on our way north.

Our destination was York. Sydney had work in the York office for a few days. This gave me time to wander its walls, visit the Viking Museum, and shop in The Shambles, that reminder of days long gone. Housing Ming was never a problem; she was happy to be in the car, even overnight, if necessary. Should the car be approached by someone she did not like the look of, she would rouse herself slowly upwards to face them. It was quite comical to see the expression of shock on the person's face, as they took a step back upon seeing the lion-like face peering out.

We had the dimensions of the rooms in our new home to hand, and had paid a large deposit on the property, with strings attached. It was to be the house in the corner with a big garden and a stone dyke running down one side. With this in mind I felt confident in looking in furniture shops with displays of carpeting, suitable for all the public areas; sitting room, dining room and hall. At Waring and Gillows, a firm I knew from my stay in Potters Bar, I was attracted to a fawn and white design, which would not show Ming's fall of hair. It was a left-over from an order from Australia, I was told, because people there were going over to bare wooden floors, just like in the house we had just left, but maybe because of the cooler climate, we put carpet down on top.

Another two months were to pass, before our house was ready for occupation, and I held out little hope of the Edinburgh branch of Waring and Gillow stocking this design and colour. The make was Brinton Lux, and practically all wool. I was missing a huge bargain, I knew. This was, however, resolved by the furniture manager. Should I buy it in total, and pay a rather big deposit, it would be delivered to the Edinburgh branch and delivered to me when requested. Sydney and I studied the dimensions of area and decided that there would be enough for the staircase as well. The total cost was below half the usual amount for this carpeting, so I was very happy with the outcome, and the manager happy to have it gone.

York gave way to Inverness, where the lads joined us [his auditors]. Here, I could make visits to my relatives in Dingwall, and visit Culloden, the place of such slaughter of clansmen in the eighteenth century. Pieces of cloth hung from the branches of the trees, that formed this sad wood, in memory of those killed in the battle. The auditors had their favourite hotels, and in Inverness, it was The Felstead, facing the river Ness. Ming chose this as her paddling place and was dubbed "The New Monster". The owners were friendly and willing to have a dog laze in their garden. They were historians of the city, and had much to say about the "Cranogs", those islands in the middle of the river, said to have been a defence against attackers and stores for food and weapons. Upon our return to Edinburgh, we made our temporary home in The Dorlin Hotel, a step across the road from Forestry Commission Headquarters, and a walk over Corstorphine hill to the property, about to become our permanent residence.

A strange situation arose at The Dorlin. A lady from the south had misrepresented her age, and should have been retired from government service for two years. This information came to me, not from Sydney, who never divulged anything regarding the confidentiality of his work. I sat with this lady having coffee, or afternoon tea, when she was disposed to let me see her vast array of garnet jewellery, hanging from her ears, and surrounding her neck and wrists. She kept telling me its value ran into thousands of pounds, but was not antique. Now, garnet is my birth stone, which I like very much for its rich red colour, but I am well aware that is not a precious stone, like a diamond or a sapphire and would never command the values quoted. Nothing was said by me to anyone, since it was the time she would be called forth to receive a gift and thanks for her many years of service. Deep down, I was sure I had been told a fantasy. It eventually emerged that she had been collecting both pay and pension plus various expenses.

The office staff was mainly made up of colleagues from Basingstoke, with some recruited from the north of England, or Scottish offices. Scientific officers were employed at The Bush, just outside Edinburgh, and near to the charming Roslin Chapel, featured in Dan Brown's book, "The Da Vinci Code". A visit to both and a walk on nearby hills, made for a good day out.

Gatherings still took place in the new office, but were never to be as open and friendly as the dinners and parties of the south. There were talks, some informative, but one was a complete disaster, its title: 'The problems of the over forties'. The talk droned on about elderly parents etc.. until Sydney excused us, saying to me — "do you know how many whiskies you've had?". I had no idea, but out of boredom I had another and then another. I was told seven. I was angry, but stone - cold sober. My usual was two and that was all I wanted; one to greet and one to be polite. It was a sulky drive home, and I backed the car up to the garage door, but did not put it inside.

We renewed our friendships with members of the Methodist Church, who lived a short distance from The Dorlin Hotel, and with others who still lived in Drumbrae. Everyone was welcoming, but we both had the feeling that things had changed. It was we who had 'moved on', whatever that means; maybe we sought new challenges. These were certainly to come, with a large garden to be laid out, and decisions to be made about the property which the builder liked to leave to the discretion of his clients.

The day arrived when we were to pick up the key to our new property from the office of our solicitor in George Street. Excitement rose, as we drove to the back entrance, via the one common entrance on to Craigcrook Road for the nine houses. The clerk of works, and other men engaged on this small development, were all quite elderly, a squad who liked to build in their traditional way, with lots of air bricks and no gimmicks. Three steps led to the covered doorway at the front, with a narrow frosted window looking towards a pathway to the street.

Inside, the vastness of hallway, sitting room and dining room made us wonder how far the carpeting would reach. Had we made an error in our calculations? Waring and Gillow came to our aid, sending someone to measure at first hand, and produce an estimate for underlay and completion of the work.

In the meantime, a colleague of Sydney's arrived in Edinburgh from York, with his wife, to look for a house to purchase. He and his family had visited us in Winchester, and would receive the same hospitality in Edinburgh, in spite of the general turmoil of our move, and bare floor boards covering the ground floor.

Johnnie was a keen amateur painter, and presented us with one of his paintings of a Scottish scene which we knew well and which would grace a wall in the dining room.

The move did not go entirely smoothly. One of the extension parts of the dining table was missing for months and, while not an immediate problem, still something to be remembered. It was discovered just in time for our house-warming party. David arrived from Durham to help out, and decide which bedroom would be his, and whether his piano had suffered any damage in the removal. It was not to be discarded - yet.

Carpets arrived, were laid, and a further piece sent from York to cover the last few steps on the staircase. I liked the turn of the stairs, with its window facing blossom trees, and its wrought iron bannister.

Our neighbours had greeted us and now were calling to make our acquaintance. Betty was first to invite me for coffee, and remark on the carpet "which seemed to go everywhere". Her husband was manager of an insurance company in the city, and her neighbour, who was about to move in, owned a large dairy, just off the Queensferry Road, and supplied most of Edinburgh with its milk and fresh cream. Kate, Bob's wife, was in charge of administering the dairy, its fleet of milk floats, all run on electricity, and its staff. People urged Bob to get computerised, but his answer was "when it can add up faster than Kate, and know that Mary down the road doesn't need milk the days she goes to visit her daughter, then I will think about it. Indeed". Kate's knowledge was phenomenal, everyone said so. Isabel and Fred had the communal road at one side of their property. Isabel, along with her sister had inherited the delicatessen, and high-class sweet shop in Davidsons Mains from their parents. As a coffee shop; it had been patronised by large numbers of Irish Navies, employed after the first world war, in upgrading the streets of Edinburgh. This corner shop had come into being when the local telephone exchange was removed from the building in nineteen twelve. Everything now sold in this shop was of the highest quality; hand-made chocolates from Perth, varieties of meats and cheeses carefully sourced, bearing appropriate price tags. This revenue provided the means for Isabel and her sister to furnish their now separate homes with beautiful chandeliers, expensive silver and landscape paintings. A dividing wall had been removed to leave a large expanse of about thirty feet by sixteen, filled with beautiful furniture.

Isabel and Fred had married late, and did not have a family. Isabel's liking for beautiful things, was just that. She did not crave admiration for her possessions, wondering why people didn't go to Jenners, the department store on Princes Street, and buy them. After attending a neighbour's wedding, several guests ended up in Isabel and Fred's house. Cars had been shared, leaving one woman in distress at being parted from her mink coat. All outdoor wear had been taken to Isabel's bedroom to be hung in the wardrobe. The guest was invited upstairs to view the coats. "It's a mink", said the guest, where upon the sliding door was opened to reveal no fewer than five mink coats "Tak' yer pick", but I think they're a' mine", which was unfortunately the case.

Gwen and Jimmy, our next door neighbours, were ballroom dancers, with a dance class run jointly. Jimmy was cooperage manager for The Scottish and Newcastle brewing company during day time. Gwen was petite, with blonde hair, and during the day, a teacher in a quite deprived district of the city. In a national dance competition in the late fifties, Gwen was voted "Ballroom Queen". Jimmy had insisted that she change her gown to all white for the competition. Yards upon yards of blue tulle was lost to the competition, but it won them prestige, and a big prize. Gwen was half French, but had been brought up in Tynecastle, a part of Edinburgh. She had been much indulged by her mother who had brought her breakfast in bed, until she rebelled at the age of fourteen. A son and daughter completed the family, the son being educated at a boarding school, not far outside Edinburgh's boundary, the daughter at a day school in the city.

Our neighbours were friendly and interesting. Next to Gwen and Jimmy, lived May and lain, a couple without children, and like Betty from "the west", Iain was also " in insurance and May, a prodigious worker for the church at Davidsons Mains, filling her freezer with cakes and flans, ready for the next church activity. She was the most generous and affable of hostesses, welcoming children and animals to her home.

Having enjoyed coffee mornings, or an evening drink with those new friends, it became clear that a house-warming party was expected. This had to include neighbours with whom we'd had little contact so far. One couple were much younger than the rest of us and were about to become a family, so they did not participate this time. He was a lawyer, and offered his firm in any need of help in the law.

Just before our move, a lively family had arrived from Selby, in Yorkshire to occupy one of the houses. The daughter of the house worked for a vet and owned her own horse, left grazing in the field behind our garden. Blue became a great pet of ours, and after a good sniffing, Ming welcomed the animal. Sydney too was besotted with Blue, of the grey coat with patches of black and a funny gait. He fed him polo mints in the morning and on his return in the evening. The horse soon knew to be waiting by the trees at the entrance to Corstorphine Hill, to receive a polo as Sydney emerged. A clap of hands would bring him racing, if at the other end of the field, legs and feet splaying out at an odd angle. Caroline's brother had joined the air force and was flying Tornadoes. He joined with us when he could, bringing us up to date with our modern fighting force. A big party was held at an hotel in Cramond to celebrate him receiving "his wings". There, I enjoyed jiving with Jimmy, quite a change from Scottish dancing. The house-warming party took place one Saturday, when David was at home and able to help. We were to be twenty two people in all, everyone seated at table. This was achieved by joining the dining table, fully extended, to the kitchen table and another table cut down in height to fit with the others. Only white sheets could cover this area, with a tartan runner from end to end.

Sixteen chairs had been moved from Duthie Terrace, and were stored in the loft. With the six chairs in daily use, seating was possible, although a bit cramped. Once set out with silver, crystal, and bowls of flowers, it looked quite stunning. Our neighbours would be augmented by some of Sydney's colleagues, so a watch had to be kept that factions mixed. The seating arrangement took care of that to a large extent. David sat near to me as my "right-hand man". Unlike Sydney, who would stand up, holding an empty bottle, saying "is there any more of this", or " the tatties are running out". David kept his eye on all and replenished the dishes with a nod, or fetched another bottle of wine from the sideboard behind Sydney. However, we could be sure that Sydney would cause riotous laughter with his anecdotes and tales about his journeys throughout Britain.

The menu was cock-a-leekie soup, with oatcakes, three large dishes of lasagne [very chic], with beans and peas for those wanting separate vegetables. Pudding was Lairds Cream, with tea or coffee and a liqueur to follow; much preparation, but easily served. Once again we launched ourselves into Edinburgh society!

The garden had to be tackled with gusto. As well as the stone dyke running down one side, where people abutting had thrown their rubbish for years, the site contained quite large stones. Mr Meikle sent his clerk of work to find out how we were getting on, and suggesting that he erect a fence to hide the dyke and its rubbish. I was aghast at the idea, thinking how lovely the wall could look, cleared of the rubbish and planted up in its crevice's with bulbs and flowers. I had already formed a circle of stones, about two feet in height, to become a compost heap in winter, and a barbeque in summer. It was easy, then to clear the composted soil and rubbish from before the dyke into the stone circle. This left a level area of good soil under the five poplar trees, growing some feet away from the dyke. It would be grassed over in the autumn and a swing hung from a branch of a poplar tree. This would be enjoyed by Gwen and myself, when we sought a time of contemplation and by of course, any visiting children.

A vegetable garden had to be established and, for the whole of the summer, Sydney laboured in trenching i.e. digging one spit and below it another. This made for excellent drainage, but was not necessary where grass was to be grown. Potatoes, the plant known to "clean" the patch gave a good crop, if somewhat late in season. I had noticed beautiful yellow raspberries growing amongst the trees where Sydney walked to work, and I walked with Ming, or not, when she would sit down at the foot of the path to wait for my return. Cuttings from the yellow rasps were easy to root and thrived beside the two rows of logan berries and varieties of cultivated raspberries.

For a bit of fun we planted some climbing gourds, to run up the drain pipe to the bathroom. Their grotesque shapes and colours drew attention as they reached to the guttering.

The Kedell Nursery in Hampshire was willing to send plants when appropriate for weather conditions in the north. We had been good customers in Winchester, and they were interested in the changes of climate from south to north. Fortunately, our site faced west, and was sheltered by the dyke and trees and bushes grown in neighbouring gardens, and our own, tall poplar trees.

Bare root fruit trees arrived in autumn from the nursery in the south; a Bramley Apple, which would grow to enormous proportions, a plum tree which was named "Golden Egg" from which, the following year, hung huge yellow plums, just like eggs, and trained over the archway to the vegetable garden. The other trees were apples; James Grieve, Charles Ross and Worcester Permain, grown as cordons along a wire fence leading to the archway. First, they were "shooched" into fine soil to await planting into their final positions. In spring the fence would be covered in blossom, in autumn, a small crop of delicious apples.

Two dozen roses arrived as ordered, on a terrible day at the beginning of November.

Queen Elizabeth of Glamis was the name, the colour a beautiful pink / slightly orange hue. They would adorn each side of the pathway leading to the front door and bloom behind the low wall facing the pavement. Sydney was away. It was the kind of rain / hail we get used to on the east coast of Scotland. I would plant as many as I could. The fear of an early frost occupied my mind. The two dozen holes I had dug the week before had filled in, but the hollows were still visible and a marker for planting. By late afternoon, I had completed planting the ones lining the pathway. It was dark, but the street light shone brightly for the final planting. I decided that would be after tea. It would have been so easy to relax by my open fire, and watch television, but I did not succumb; instead, dressed in my "dog walking" gear I faced the elements, which was now heavy rain and strong wind. Few people passed, and some remarked that I could find something better to be doing. With rain now pouring down, the risk of frost receded. The result was a beautiful line-up next summer.

In the front lawn the builder had planted a Rowan tree, which was watered most days by an ex German aircraft pilot who had many tales of his exploits during the War. In spite of my offers to water the tree, he would not allow it. He was one of Mr Meikie's elite staff of older staff who constructed houses in the old way wooden plank floors, no expensive frills, and plenty vents. Although the fields behind the properties, belonged to Mr Meikle, he refused to build there. His retired clerk of works looked over the fields to Craigcrook Castle and it would "spoil his view and Mr Gray would not like that." Besides, the children used the steeper fields to sledge and ski down.

The hidden burn took its route alongside the dyke, and sometimes its gurgling could be heard near the roadway, where it ran in a culvert to the "marley pits" on the opposite side of the road. This was an area where pebbles had been dug out over many years. It could be quite swamp like, and unstable for building.

Eventually, it was drained and pile driven, so that houses could be built on floating foundations, apparently.

A flood did occur in the field, just beyond our fence. Mr Law, now clerk of works, came to tell us that a drain would be dug alongside our driveway to empty the water into the street drain. On the other hand, Mr Meikle said it could be led into our garden, so that we could have a garden pool, and then drained into the burn. At this stage, it seemed too much to take on, and we let the offer pass. It became a favourite place for seagulls. They arrived in mass to swim around in their temporary pond.

Charoley bullocks occupied the fields as far as the path to the hill. They could be playful, but tolerant of Ming, except for one. I was on top of a mound, when a confrontation arose. He had breached the far fence, and was approaching Ming in a steady, threatening way. By this time, I was screaming, as each plodded towards the other. I raced forward to save my dog, by what means, I knew not. As I made up the few hundred yards to the encounter, the bullock turned to retreat, Ming slowly in pursuit, with chest stuck out. This, I came to understand, as her method of seeing off offenders. Four Jack Russells, when met in the wood, clamoured round her, jumping and squealing as she pressed forward on them, and they retreated, and she could sit down in peace. Her enormous coat was part of this defence.

Sometimes, the cattle congregated in a corner of the field just outside our fence. We had a planted Brussel sprouts there, with permission, of course and at the suggestion of our kind property developer. I watched a bullock pull one out by its roots and swallow it whole, roots earth, all. It was a day on which some of the animals had broken a field fence and had trodden over the front gardens newly established; not appreciated by the owners who guided them with difficulty back into a field and placed a barricade at the break in the fence.

Visits to The Bush, the experimental centre for The Forestry Commission and Ministry of Agriculture were always of interest.

Any new project could be intriguing. It was here that I was surprised to see a hedge of Lawson Cypress, no more than ten inches in width. This was achieved by each branch growing beyond this measurement being cut off, and only branches growing sideways being encouraged.

A Lawson Cypress hedge had been rejected by me, as being too untidy, but on seeing this hedge at The Bush, I took on the challenge and ordered two hundred Saplings required to line the fence and driveway at the back of the house. They came at a knock-down price, and a warning of the difficult task I had taken on. Sydney and I dug holes, and planted our forest. It was easy, to start with, cutting off offending branches that grew outward. Upward growth was fast, and within five years, I could be seen teetering on the top of a ladder, attacking the greenery from both top and side. It was worth all the effort, shielding the garden from north winds.

The area behind the garage was grassed over and received items to be discarded, or cut up, as in the case of huge branches brought down from the hill, by Sydney on his way home. To give interest to that side wall of the house, with its chimney breast, I planted a Russian vine which soon edged up the white pebble-dash wall and was a riot of reds and oranges in autumn. Some of the houses were rendered with Norwegian pebble-dash, making the walls sparkle in sunlight. The outlet to the baxi fire was on this wall, so that to clear the ashes, I could lift out the bin and scatter them on the compost circle.

Spring came late, and thoughts of bulbs in full bloom and flowers which would not thrive this far north were a frustration; so much so, that I found myself in the wood one day weeping to be back in Winchester, exchanging cuttings with my friends, and enjoying a springtime, yet to arrive in Edinburgh. This garden was completely flat, so that any rockery would have to be constructed. Stones were plentiful, and of a good size for making an interesting shape, rather than just a mound. In front of the dining room window, I dug out a small pond, which I lined with a waterproof layer. It fitted well and was made deep enough for fish to survive the winter. This enabled me to grow some pond plants and creepers around the edge, making this a bit of a feature all year round. A surprise came to us, the first spring of our occupation. In the garden of an older house beyond the dyke, five cherry trees came into blossom. We had missed seeing the fruit which covered the ground each autumn, and brought a variety of birds to feed.

Some years later, I had lifted my small neighbour over a wire fence by the dyke, to go to the swing. After that she was often on the first wire, with arms outstretched wanting to come over, in particular to visit the fish. Being aware of her safety, we constructed a wire mesh cover for the pool, so that, should she succeed in scaling the fence or crawling through she would be 'safe'. Gate fastenings were too high for her to reach.

When David left for Durham University, we received a request from Hampshire Council, that we house a student where we were, in place of him. Edinburgh was scarce of student accommodation, to the extent that some students were sleeping in church halls, some fifteen miles beyond its boundary. We contacted the university, and Mrs Sim took our names and sent rules of engagement, so to speak. They would mainly be post-graduates unless relatively local; Perth, Dundee. The first girls to arrive, I wanted two together to make things easier all round, were Scottish, one from Kirkaldy. Her mother would come to inspect the premises, and this person duly appeared. She turned over the duvet in the bed her daughter would occupy. The dog was not an issue. We accepted the girls into our home on a temporary basis, and according to our rules of no visitors in bedrooms, home by eleven o' clock unless told in advance, and a late night call if stranded, for me or Sydney to come to their aid.

Of the eight students we welcomed, only these Scots were a problem. One girl wore a T shirt announcing 'I'm Free'. On the first night of their stay, our neighbour called to tell us a fracas was in progress on the pavement outside our house. It was now after eleven o'clock, and Sydney went out. He sent the boys packing and marched the girls up the path into the house. The following two nights were normal, and we thought they had settled down, but the third night they did not appear at all. Mrs Sim was contacted and we were released of any obligation. Their clothes and books were collected along with a note of apology from the university. We were told that they were living somewhere in the Spottiswood area of Edinburgh. Some months later, a distraught aunt of the girl from Kirkcaldy, telephoned to ask had we an address for either girl. The caller was referred to Mrs Sim, who rang to say the two were missing from all her records. It was a bad beginning.

Nine

The next guests were one German and one American. This proved to be a most rewarding association. Renatta arrived at the front door, tall, slim and with short reddish hair. Her first words were "I run, where to go twenty five kilometres?". I brought her in and showed her the room which would be hers and tried to explain our set-up. After drawing a map of the route to Cramond, and out to Queensferry, with the option of taking the ferry over the river Almond, and returning by the main road, it seemed an equivalent mileage. Renatta proved to be a good friend, powerful in the garden with a spade, and climbing the ladder to the loft to bring down chairs when a party had been arranged. Her companion was Amy, an American girl with a strong sense of responsibility towards those less fortunate than herself. A bond soon grew up between the girls. We could hear laughter, or footsteps coming from one room, as they joined together for studies or listen to music on their radios. It became clear that Renatta took the lead in most of their activities together. In spite of her difficulty in using a foreign language, it was she who brought back timetables for bus or train journeys, and applied for tickets for university events. Language soon became no barrier for Renatta. Her command and focus came to the fore. I overheard a remark made to Amy, on one visit by my mother, "Do you not just wish you were German?".

Only breakfast had to be fed to the girls. Other meals were provided at the university. Of course, my kettle was always available, alongside a tin of baking or biscuits. Each Friday, I placed a bill for £1.50 at their places at table, believing that a small gesture of cost should be made. The experience of having the girls to stay had been one of interest and delight. Their last kindness to me was when they cleared away all the items from a dinner party I was having, served coffee, to my guests, washed up by hand, even the spare chairs were back in the loft. I was "Renatta's Scottish mother", Amy wrote from Guatemala, where she was caring for very poor and deprived children. Both sent Christmas cards for some years.

Summer intervened, before Mrs Sim arranged for another two girls to be lodged with us. Both were Malayan, very serious, and kept themselves very much to themselves, studying in their own rooms. My invitations to sit by the open fire and watch a bit of television were never taken up. They left, thanking me nicely for their stay, but I was never allowed to enter their world. Next came a law student and a medical student, both English. The lawyer never seemed to have any work, and was keen to accept any diversion from work that I could provide. She walked Ming in the woods, chatted with the neighbours, and read my "Scotsman". I introduced her to the neighbour of the cherry trees, in case they knew of any work that would interest her. Both were lawyers, and the husband also a chartered accountant, in business with his brother. By chance, I was also able to let her meet the wife of a lawyer two doors away, whose firm was wide-ranging in all aspects of the law. It seemed odd to find such apathy in one so young, since she claimed to be looking for work at the end of the year. Later, I was to discover that she was part of a very affluent border family, whose brother had excelled at university, leaving her with an inferiority feeling, and little academic drive. "She would soon be married, anyway". By contrast, the doctor was always pressed for time. She was beset on every side by deadlines, or some extra study she wanted to pursue. Hardly ever was she seen walking in the wood, or meeting Sydney on his way home. The garden and my swing, seemed to be her only distraction from her studies. Even after the university had closed for the summer, she asked if she could stay with us during most of August. This did not cause us any inconvenience. She had a key, and mostly cooked her own food, when not eating out. Her home was in the south of England, and she had set her sights on working in one of the big London hospitals.

Kate and Judy were both Americans, from Oregon and Minneapolis. Again they were big in contrast. This time one enjoyed the indulgence of a wealthy family, the other what looked like extreme poverty. My mother, who had been in America a few times sensed this immediately. She knew how everything had to be paid for. Judy did have a bursary, and did not have to pay tuition fees, but other expenses were hard to bear. As far as we could, Sydney tried to mitigate Judy's situation without insult. Immediately university was out, she returned to her Jewish family somewhere in Oregon.

Kate also returned to America, but the following year was arranging for her family to visit Scotland, and asking for my help in this. For the first two nights they would be our guests, parents, grandma, while Kate spent that time with a friend. I had booked them all into The King James Hotel, near to both railway station and bus station, and where I knew there would be a programme of Scottish entertainment for three evenings. Edinburgh took up all of their time, before hiring a car and moving north. I had booked them two nights in Stirling, and they were much amused at seeing the sign for Crook of Devon, where someone had painted "twinned with the thief of Baghdad". They were anxious to stay in Inverness, which would not have been my choice, but I booked them into The Felstead, the small hotel by the river Ness, where Sydney and his team of auditors often lodged and where I knew they would receive a warm welcome, and glean information. Maybe the tales of the monster and Urquhart Castle would fire their imagination. The journey by car to the Kyle of Lochalsh had been tricky, with only passing places in parts, and wild open country on both sides. This was an emotional prelude to their visit to the Isle of Skye, where I had again advance-booked, keeping my fingers crossed that it was the right location for them. Grandma's forebears had been driven from the island during the clearances "to make room for sheep". She had read widely on the subject, and was able to pin-point the croft area occupied by her family, and now with the stones of its building half buried in the rough grass.

Back in Edinburgh, visits were made to the Borders, to Glasgow, and to The Edinburgh Crystal shop at Penicuik, where crystal was packed to be sent home, without VAT being charged. On the last evening, Sydney and I were invited to The King James for dinner with them, where our friend, lain McPhail and his band, were providing the music for the evening. All male diners were invited to lift " The Man hood Stone" which as it suggests was a boys test for entry into manhood. All was easy until Sydney's turn, when it suddenly became so heavy no one could move it. Gales of laughter arose, and four men appeared to drag it behind a screen. Photographs were taken of Kate's grandmother holding a set of bagpipes to her mouth. Before leaving, we were presented with a pewter tray made in America, in thanks for our help, and an invitation to visit them one day. A month later, a parcel arrived. Inside was a brass plaque, extolling us as Scotland's most efficient tour guides, Scotland's finest ambassadors of good will. Edinburgh's most gracious hosts. A feeling of worthiness swept over us and we nodded our pleasure at such recognition.

The following year, Mrs Sim rang to say that accommodation for students had eased, with a whole street on the south side of the city being converted into bed sits for students and young people. Sydney and I were invited to view what had been done.

David arrived home, having been diagnosed with a back condition, and was sent to hospital. It was not his first visit to The Royal Infirmary. While on a visit from Durham, he collapsed with a perforated appendix. His Greek friend, amongst others, was instrumental in getting him emergency help. While still in Winchester, we received a call "I'm in hospital in Edinburgh in hospital, sorry I'm going to be sick". A follow-up call explained the situation. We assumed his car was in Edinburgh.

The journey north was so well-known to us, and only to Edinburgh. To travel overnight, I went to sleep after tea, and took the first leg, up to "the Watford Gap". It seemed to be my habit to be fully awake at eleven o'clock, if not in bed. By ten thirty, with the car packed, we were ready to set off. Margaret would look after Ming and the house during our absence.

David was well-looked after in hospital, by a nurse from Winchester. When he left after some days in the convalescent hospital, he felt he had to bid her farewell. This meant parking both cars at the hospital, for the twenty minutes allowed. During this time, an ambulance hit the back of our quite new Cortina. Only the boot really suffered damage, and with a length of strong string holding it shut, we decided to make the journey back to Winchester, and have the repair done at 'The Hyde Abbey'. This was not the end of our trials. Approaching Jedburgh, David ordered the car to be stopped. He had espied an American student with whom he was particularly friendly, sitting on the verge by his car. I drew up to find David jumping out and running back to greet his friend. I expected another collapse, but it did not happen. It was a happy interlude. The traffic was such that my car was always in view from the others behind. For miles, I had trailed three articulated lorries in convoy, and getting fed up, decided to overtake. Three together is a big undertaking, and with lights flashing from behind, I missed the M18 where

I intended to turn off. I let Sydney overtake me, so that I could follow him off the motorway at the next opportunity. That came at the slip road from Rotherham and since we had planned one stay for the night, it was in The Earl of Strafford Hotel.

I had to be suitably contrite about my impatient action earlier. The incident was brought up on many occasions in the future. David made a good recovery.

Unbeknown to us, David had been suffering from a back problem, worsened by his training in the university hockey team. Friends had been half-carrying him downstairs to lectures. He was seen by the university doctor, and X rays were taken. Term ended, and he returned to Edinburgh, to be investigated at Saint Rafael's hospital. The bursar at Durham had kindly sent the results to the hospital, so that they would not be duplicated. A diagnosis of spondylolisthesis was given to David on his own, with the option of an operation, but might end up in a wheelchair as a result; some statement for a young hockey player to absorb! A further opinion was sought, and a soft brace made to protect the back from quick, unusual movement for two months.

During this time, David was not idle. He coached some pupils for their Higher Certificates in Mathematics. Later on he found himself in a temporary post in The Forestry Commission, so that he and Sydney left together most mornings, for the walk over the hill, down through the Zoo to the office on the opposite side of the Glasgow Road. This proved a good way to convalesce, but coming at such a price. It meant a year away from studies, the loss of day to day, friendships which had been built up over the past two years, a feeling of being left out, although never expressed. Going back to try to gather up the threads of where he had left off must have been very hard. Instead of going forward, and celebrating with well-known students at the end of three years, he found himself at a new beginning, with people he did not know. It was with relief and admiration that Sydney and I spent two days in Durham, standing on the Palace Green, after graduation and joining in the celebrations afterwards, with some of his new companions and their families.

David did not want to pursue a life in academia, and decided to become a chartered accountant. He was accepted by a firm in London, so for him, at least, it was back to the south of England.

Before leaving, the three of us spent a week in The Highlands, exploring Glen Affric and admiring the water falls. It is also memorable for meeting a couple of girls from Glasgow, high up in the glen, still in flip flops. They remarked on the gale that was almost blowing us off our feet, and the fact that they would have been better with shoes on in case they went sprawling.

David secured for himself a one room flat in West Hampstead, with its own front door, and steps at the back down to the garden. This room had two single beds, washing facilities and was adequate, since much of his time was spent in work outside London.

There was one minor problem. David needed his orthopaedic mattress. Against everyone else's advice, I decided it could be sent by rail, but its dimensions did not comply with the railway service. It looked like having to be termed "removal". However, by the time I had it roped up, and perhaps ruined it, because of being bent round, it was accepted for transporting by rail, and arrived intact, ready for use.

Thus my connection with student life ended. I missed my association with the children at Greenacres, but kept in touch with Freda, its Scottish dancing headmistress. Once she came with her mother to stay, but mostly called on us when visiting the west of Scotland. She had learned quite a lot of Gaelic during her travels, and was not easily overcharged; "charge the old bags three pounds extra", was soon brought down to the amount the locals were paying.

The director of special schools in Edinburgh, was pleased by my offer of two days a week at one of his schools. He tentatively teased out the work being done in Hampshire and decided that children were the same, with the same needs, while backgrounds could be very different. Indeed, the contrast was quite stark. Most families, with a child at Greenacres were affluent, with brothers and sisters who could make such a difference to the progress of the handicapped brother or sister.

Gogarburn was a hospital-school where many children could never benefit from formal education. Most of the children attending school went home each day or at weekends, with the hospital as a back-up, if required.

An introduction was arranged, and I was taken to Gogarburn to meet Mrs Carlin, the headmistress, and see around school and hospital, where many of the wards were "Closed wards". I was allocated to the wise and kindly Mrs Ross, wife of the Dean of the Faculty of Divinity at Edinburgh University. Memories of my brief time spent there came rushing back. This was to be my new 'Greenacres', and on Monday I would meet the seven pupils who made up Mrs Ross's class, and who sorely needed one to one attention most of the time " Immediately, I felt welcomed into the class by the four boys and three girls, and faced a barrage of questions from the more vocal element.

Assembly took place two days a week, when a visiting lady from church took the service. "Give me joy in my heart" was the favourite hymn, when even those without speech reacted with hands or heads shaking. One boy got down under the piano, which mystified the teachers, until it was guessed that he could feel the beat and vibration of Mrs Robb's playing. Children were brought in wheelchairs by a nurse, and others in small groups, with a chaperone. One or two were allowed to cross the grass to school by themselves. Boundaries were secured by unobtrusive wire fencing, and gates with complicated latches. This did not mean that pupils never breached those defences. The school was alerted one day to the fact a that a pupil was standing on the bridge which crosses the busy M8 route to Glasgow, taking her clothes off and throwing them down on the rush hour traffic, quite a dangerous antic. Happily no accident resulted, and the girl was able to explain that a man going through the gate, had let her go first. She of course wanted her clothes back, but settled for being wrapped in a warm blanket and returned, cold, to her ward for a hot drink before school.

Flexibility and encouragement were the keynotes of our care. Eyes had to be wide open to see a potential here or an interest there to be developed to advantage. The mini bus which brought children who lived at home to school each day was widely used on outings. One girl was picked up from a deprived district, the garden high in long grass and weeds, and the back door kicked in, with a board covering the hole. Opposite was a house which stood out in contrast to the others, with their neglected paths and unkempt appearance. When asked about this garden, the reply came "anyone setting foot on that garden would hae their heed bashed in". There were three quite scary men who lived there with their mother, who liked flowers and a tidy garden. Outings were made to Leith and Granton harbours where ships could be viewed, and admired. A cafe' on Leith Walk was our destination, where staff and pupils were most welcome. Our class of near teenagers, drew pictures or pasted pictures in thanks to the owners of this cafe' for their generous hospitality, where no payment was taken.

Our entourage of wheelchairs and excited children was also welcomed at the vast shopping mall at The Gyle, near to the school. There, the men in charge of this open space, lined with shops and attractions, were most helpful, holding a wheelchair when someone strayed and had to be brought back to the group; sometimes issuing a firm reprimand on return. Always, we were given money for our charges; one thing which stood out on these outings, was the generosity of passers-by, when seeing our little group. One girl had to be clamped to a member of staff. She cherished babies, and would dash over to any pram which came her way. We tried various means of distraction from this habit, by providing dolls, and even a pram, which could be taken home at weekends, but to no avail. Her other penchant was for shiny objects. When her parents were about to welcome guests for a special dinner, and she had to be taken home for some reason, upon seeing the crystal and lighted candles she reached out and grabbed the table cloth, bringing food, silver, lighted candles crashing to the floor. The episode at least brought home to the guests, mostly educationalists, how unpredictable such children's behaviour could be, and why it was impossible to have them live at home all the time. It is so difficult to connect with a fourteen year old, whose mind equates to that of young child.

Being small of stature, I often had to shorten frocks or skirts, and it struck me that some pupils might be interested in the process. This turned out to be the case, and when I brought in my sewing machine, it was Colin, a most disruptive pupil, who enjoyed it most. Of course as soon as his attention span ended, he wanted to race it to hear the noise. At home, I had some square samples of curtain material, which I thought could be made into some patchwork. This became popular, and produced the end product of a cushion or a bag. Colin enjoyed lashing out at anyone in passing, and it was felt that his time with the sewing machine, and many threats about racing it, helped to calm his urge to hurt others, and instead, concentrate on what could be a nice gift for someone.

Jenners, the large department store on Princes Street, was most generous to our parties, on their visits to the store, keeping us supplied with samples for patchwork. After Christmas, the school was offered the choice of decorations taken down. Gogarburn must have been the best dressed school in Edinburgh, each year, as we sifted through our store of greenery and baubles from the previous year.

An announcement was made that Gogarburn was to receive a very special visitor. She was Mrs Thatcher. The reception would not be at school, but aboard a canal boat, with some of the children, and at her request not picked out for their good behaviour. A ballot was held, and both Colin and his brother emerged. In some ways Colin's brother was the more difficult to manage. For some time before the event, Cathy, the hospital matron in charge of the visit, nurtured the children in what would happen on the day. Knowing that Mrs Thatcher would be carrying a handbag, a member of staff was lined up with others for a practice run of introduction and handshaking with a handbag. All went well until the day before Mrs Thatcher's arrival, when Colin's brother grabbed someone else's handbag and whacked Cathy on the stomach. He said it was O.K. because she wasn't the "special lady". I did not accompany the sail, but heard how Mrs Thatcher had related to the children, and how everyone admired her happy and encouraging remarks to the staff. Gardening, like sewing, was to become another extra mural activity. Sydney came one afternoon and dug out a patch for us, which we could view from the classroom window. It was to be planted up with vegetables, and some flowers for next summer. The boy best at digging and planting was one I was told, it was not quite safe to be left alone with. He loved to rake and tidy up. We got on well, but I was careful not to enter the open shed where we kept tools. Mrs Ross always told him she would be 'watching from the window'.

Paul liked fire, and in particular men's pipes, and when Sydney lit up his pipe on collecting me one afternoon, he sang and danced around, asking each day after that if Sydney was smoking his pipe and wearing his kilt, which seemed to be another obsession. He was not allowed near fires or anything likely to be set alight. Out and about, he had to be prevented from accosting a man smoking a pipe or wearing a kilt, which would be grabbed and swung from side to side with an accompanying Scottish tune, ra-ra-ra-rara to the amusement of one man, but to the distress of a woman walking with her husband recovering from a stroke. This encounter was at Cramond beach, but her view that boys like Paul should not be allowed out in public seemed a bit extreme.

The school took very serious notice of comments about the children when taken out into the community. An embarrassment to carers and small annoyance to the public, was carefully weighed against the controlled freedom of contact outside school. Just as young people were encouraged into further education, so it was with our charges. Although lacking the potential of others, our boys in particular were keen to be young men. They rough and tumbled and copied the actions of any workmen coming to the school, showing off and boasting when given a piece of equipment to hold or pass. The girls, too benefited from the extra time at school, developing their innate instinct to look after small children, and care about hair and appearance.

The toilet block was in the middle of the wooden building which was now the school. It had been built just after the first world war to house those suffering from tuberculosis. The toilet block was open to the elements, and assistants found it very cold in winter, when taking a child in a wheelchair to the toilet. Talk had gone on amongst the staff about conditions in the block, but concerned that a complaint would jeopardise their job. It was obvious who needed to be the "sacrificial lamb". I started by writing to my local councillor, who rang up to say he didn't know such a school existed, but would pass on my letter to the Education Department in Torphichen Street.

I was invited to a meeting in a council office on King George 1V Bridge. It is memorable for me in that Robin Cook the late M.P. was coming down the steps, greeting me with a shake of the head, and handshake of sympathy. Inside the vestibule, a girl behind a desk indicated that I take a seat along the wall. Three other persons entered, holding clip boards, and sat by one of the doors. A man came out to ask if Mrs Cruden was here, and I followed him into a large office facing the street, with the other three behind me.

I was interrogated as to my status at this school, which no one seemed to know much about, and about the school in

Hampshire. Much writing went down on clipboards, and eventually, I was asked to describe the nature of my complaint. I decided to answer in the vernacular, quoting some of the expressions of disgust at the prevailing conditions. Most of this was not written down, and I left with an assurance that the matter would receive due attention. To everyone's surprise it did, and the following week men arrived to enclose the area and put in a radiator. A new ramp was to built for easier access by wheelchairs, and the headmistress was instrumental in bringing the cost of this down from one thousand pounds to two hundred, if carried out by "hospital maintenance" rather than put out to contract.

Colin liked to be in the garden, but his interest in plants was zero, while insects, especially ladybirds, were sought and watched for long stretches of his feeble concentration span. By accident, I had him under control, if I wore my high-heeled boots. One day sitting together, he threw something. I stood up inadvertently stamping on his foot. In spite of all my apologies, he was to ask me each time we met if I would not hit his foot if he was good.

Sports Day at Gogarburn was a feat of imagination by the staff. Parents were invited, and saw another side of their child's development, and they could discuss their situation with others in a similar position. It was an opportunity for teachers, and assistants, to learn more about a child's background, without having to ask too many questions; each year, a jolly occasion. Wheelchairs got stuck in grass, one boy leapt over the high fence surrounding the school and couldn't get back in. There was a maypole and races for the adults. Everyone received a ribbon.

I was once again to be the recipient of a gift from The Rotary Club, this time, the Edinburgh one. At the Christmas party, Santa arrived on his sleigh, bells ringing and music playing, with gifts for each child, and for volunteers of school and hospital.

In later years The Royal Bank of Scotland would buy the area, upon which to build their prestigious new headquarters. The cherry tree, brought as a sapling from our next door garden in

Craigcrook Road, was the only reminder of our garden behind the school.

David Gwen, Jean, Kate and Bob's daughter, and Fred, all living in "The Row" had birthdays early in August. Apart from Hogmanay and Burns Night, this was the main gathering of neighbours in the year. It took place in our garden or in the countryside near Peebles. Bob led the convoy of four cars in his Rolls Royce which was a present to himself, after some liaison with Canadian distributers, which saved money by some component he had introduced to them The Rolls also ran on two Star petrol!

This was not a simple outing. Deck chairs, tables, exotic food and a tantalus had to be unpacked, and set out near the river at Innerleithen. Rounders was the game played, and taken very seriously, men against women, until exhaustion set in. I had been tempted to enter the water on some occasions, when the ball landed on the far side of the river.

I was able to do this when I discovered my sandals were made of plastic, so could counter the men's greater strength in reaching the far bank. The Rolls Royce attracted some attention when parked, but Bob answered the questions, saying that he didn't know much about it; that his boss let him use it at weekends. Sometimes, we ended our outing at The Peebles Hydro, which suited Gwen, whose penchant was not for the open air, but rather the dance floor of The Hydro, where her blonde hair, petite figure and expertise on the dance floor brought her many admirers from amongst the guests, staying there. A visit to any fish and chip shop open on our way home, brought more comment on our lead transport. The day ended in Kate's vast sitting room with small portions of fish and chips and an extra- large dram. Kate did not do small drams.

The highlight of our gatherings came with the wedding of Princess Diana and Prince Charles. Tentatively, Sydney and I started the building of a bonfire in the field behind our back garden. We had branches from the poplars and lots of old bush stumps, so it grew. Word got around, and people from father away brought their contribution.

Towards the end, Bob sent a lorry load of spare pallets to bolster the bonfire. Neighbours took down most of the construction, and built it up in layers, with a hole for any escaping animal and a means of lighting it safely.

Some guests joined our neighbours for a treasure hunt in our garden, with food and games. This time our Chinese neighbours came along expressing amazement at our antics to begin with. My piece-de-resistence in the treasure hunt was "a tree growing twelve feet above any soil". Two people spotted it, growing out of a bole in one of the poplars far above ground.

Ten

CLIMAX OF THIS HISTORIC DAY CAME WITH THE LIGHTING OF the bonfire. Sydney was accorded this privilege, and found a long branch which would reach right into the base. Safety had to be of prime importance. There were cloths at the base soaked in petrol, to give it a good start. No hitches occurred during lighting, and we could hear the sound of crackling as it started to blaze. It was indeed spectacular and, apparently seen from the north side of the hill, competing successfully with the official bonfires lit around the city. Only petrified organic matter was left where its base had been, but we dowsed it well before it became part of the field again.

The pastime of Scottish Country Dancing became paramount in our recreational interests. Already members of The Scottish Country Dance Society, we were faced with a plethora of rules about classes of all stages of age and competence, of events, and competitions, ranging far and wide. We bought the booklet listing names and addresses of secretaries throughout the world. It was obvious, that no matter where in the world you were, you would be in reach of a dance club. Nearly all teachers went back to the days of Miss Milligan and Mrs Stewart, who collected remembered dances and written dances from old ball programmes. A handbook was issued entitled, 'One hundred and one Scottish Dances', first published in nineteen fifty six, and with comprehensive instructions on figures and timing. Miss Margaret Brown was taking a class for intermediate dancers, and asked us to join and be of help. She was mild with the class, compared with her competition partner, brought in sometimes to raise standards. A hand offered too low or a toe not pointed correctly, he pounced on straight away. One girl of fourteen, who left nothing to be desired in her expertise, and whom we met at competitions, chose Sydney as her mentor. Small upsets about adjudications, or advice she had received during a competition were brought to him.

My sister-in-law upon opening the front door, found the girl declaring "I must see Syd". He was not at home and I would not do as his replacement. "I'll just wait then.". The matter was not connected with dancing, so she was advised to raise the matter of some boyfriend with her father.

The Music Festival attracted many participants, during a week of competitions. The last Saturday was given over to Scottish Country Dancing in the beautiful Assembly Rooms in George Street. The morning and much of the afternoon, was given over to children's competitions, and it was here that Sydney came into his own, much in demand to fix sashes, look for a lost slipper, or find out the time of a performance.

Jim Johnstone of Dumfries put two teams of eight girls forward for the competition. Their teacher was given a choice of two dances to be performed. Stirling was also represented, along with teams from towns and villages around Edinburgh. In the seventies, over a thousand excited children were competitors each year. As well as being scribe for the nimble and expert dancer, who adjudicated, I was often asked to demonstrate a step, or explain a formation to the audience of parents. Teachers waited anxiously for their adjudication sheets to be released, with the marks and places allocated. Sydney now became the comforter of those falling below their expected results, and congratulator of those who excelled. Time did not allow for eating out, so I volunteered meals for scribes, adjudicators, and stewards, about sixteen people in all. My jam pan, covered with a sheet sat in the boot of the car, with a pot of cooked rice. I had made a huge beef casserole which could easily be shared and served up. There was a cooker and electric kettle in the kitchen for our use. People came and went, serving themselves and making tea or coffee as they relaxed from their duties.

By mid-afternoon, the audience was somewhat depleted, parents leaving for an afternoon's shopping in Edinburgh. Most thanked us and remarked on the building and its beautiful ballroom, with mirrors at each end reflecting the chandeliers.

The evening was reserved for adult teams of dancers, culminating in a free programme for a special trophy, 'The Cusson's Cup', donated by Cussons, the soap manufacturing firm, and much treasured by the winner. Teams from Aberdeen and Glasgow were common, but once a team from Stoke Podges gave the local teams an incredible challenge. Unheard of ladies came dressed in coloured gowns, with sashes of course, and their partners in matching shirts. This was met with mixed feelings, that traditional white had been abandoned, but had it detracted from the quality of the dance was a moot question. Sydney was asked to bring forth the coveted trophy from its locked cupboard, so that the winners could be photographed holding it, before its return to locked custody, for another year.

An annual ball was held by The Royal Scottish Country Dance Society [country, meaning contra, couples facing partners], in The Assembly Rooms, this magnificent building replacing its predecessor in Assembly Close, just off The Royal Mile. An elderly member at such an event, ticked off any male dancer, already in shirt sleeves, in anticipation of heat to be generated, to put his coat back on. After two dances, she mounted the rostrum to announce "Gentlemen may now remove their jackets ". Very few did, and there was little time for drinks between dances. Ladies fared better, in their long sleeveless gowns. Guests, from the hotel opposite were intrigued to see ladies thus attired sitting on the granite steps, fanning themselves in mid-winter.

The church hall at Cramond, was where Alec Milligan held his club on Saturday evenings. He was Miss Milligan's nephew, founder of The Society, and Milligan from his other parent. Although a splendid dancer, and having gained certificates from The Society, he quickly left, feeling that while it had put the kilt, and dancing on the world map, its changes were often at odds with tradition, which he was keen to uphold.

'Dancing Forth' was a performance put on in The George Square Theatre, by The Society. It presented dancing, music and comedy to suit all tastes. One year, we employed a professional director, Joe Cassiano and his assistant, Eve. This proved a great asset in practical terms, in stage management and structures, and timing, to be followed by ourselves in future.

Our chairman was escorting a young Japanese lady, the cast thought, but soon they were to be married. Atsuku's family visited Scotland, and commissioned a CD, by a popular band, so that if a band was not available, we would still have the music.

Edinburgh was still a popular city for our friends from both north and south to visit. My younger sisters enjoyed a day trip with tea in Jenners and an early train back to Aberdeen. Friends and neighbours from Winchester came to stay with us, on their way to adventures in The Highlands or on their return journey to the south. We had to be ready with maps and full of information to answer their many questions. Visiting the Tattoo, was always a 'must' if at the right time.

My young ex-neighbour came to Edinburgh on his own at the age of twelve. His mother took him to Victoria Coach station, and put him aboard a coach for Edinburgh, in the care of the coach company. Sydney and I met him at the coach Station, with his notebook filled with names of towns and places he had passed through. Apparently, passengers had been kind and he had sat in different seats with permission from the conductor.

It was then that I had to arrange a suitable itinerary of things to do, and places to visit. One obvious place was the newly opened Forth Bridge, so on Sunday, the three of us set out to cross on foot. A pathway across the bridge had just been opened. About midway across, three familiar figures approached. Sydney nudged our guest, who became suitably astonished as he realized it to be our neighbours from Abbots Ann Road, with Hamish, their son, just a few years older than himself. They had moved to Edinburgh sometime before us, when The Commission moved to its new headquarters.

David's friends from school days also appeared from time to time. One New Year, two friends were coming from the south to spend it with us. Snow had been falling all day, and by six o'clock, it was a "white out". An eery silence had fallen on the city, and no transport was running, no taxis were available and we couldn't take the car out. David got out his sledge, and set out for Waverley Station, some three miles distant, in the hope that their train would arrive on time. It did and eventually the boys arrived at the house, with their luggage on the sledge, tired and cold. The journey called for a "wee dram", and after pie and chips, the boys were glad to retire, looking forward to the next day which was New Years Eve.

Usual preparations were in hand. Tables were joined together, in the dining room, and laid up for eighteen people to have breakfast. It was always uncertain, what number would see it through to breakfast. On this occasion Sydney and I did not attend the ball, The Society held each year in Trinity School, but Sydney did dress in kilt and full regalia, as the evening demanded. He carried his bottle of 'malt' to the neighbour who that year was hosting dinner for everyone, including David's friends. Breakfast was always at our house, but Hogmanay dinner was rotated by the others, as was buffet lunches on second and third of January. The young men played their part, clearing snow from the pavement in front of our houses and taking Ming for a walk when the snow stopped.

Excitement rose as nine o'clock approached, when we were expected next door for our Hogmanay dinner. Just before midnight I returned with one of the boys, to collect a present he had forgotten. Time overtook us, silence prevailed as we realised the moment of midnight was upon us. A bright moon skidded across the sky, and suddenly fireworks were speeding upwards and exploding in a spray of colour. The sound of ships' horns reached our ears from the port of Leith, in welcome to the New Year. I wished him all the luck and happiness in the following year, and as I turned to make sure the front door was properly locked, he whispered "that was magic, I shall never forget it".

He, of course, was welcomed by the diners as "the first foot", and urged to open his bottle of whisky for the company to drink a toast to the New Year. The night progressed with visits to each house, fun, games and a bit of dancing, culminating in breakfast at our house. Again, the boys stepped forward. Using two frying pans, they soon had eggs, sausages, already cooked, and bacon served up with hot pancakes and toast.

Some people did not come to breakfast, but were replaced by their sons or daughter, who had been elsewhere, but knew where breakfast would be served around eight thirty.

Sydney's work took him to offices all over the country. Where there was a dance club, he packed his kilt, and I accompanied him on many occasions. York, Inverness, Aberdeen were our favourite destinations. Some of his young accountants studied their courses at Cambridge, and I took the opportunity of going there in order to see The Book of Deer, an ancient manuscript, brought from Pluscarden Abbey in Aberdeenshire. It was brought out and shown to me, with some reluctance as to why I should want to see it, which begged the question why it should remain in the university library of Cambridge, and not in The Museum of Antiques in Edinburgh.

My adventures during the day, were investigated by the team at dinner in the evening. One day, while staying at an hotel, just outside Ross-on-Wye, I decided to visit Gloucester by public transport. I boarded a bus taking passengers uphill, past fields of woolly sheep to some houses surrounding a large barn. Everyone dismounted and went into the barn, so I followed the other seven people. Sheering was in progress. Greetings were exchanged, and I was nodded to. The operation was overseen by a tall man, really tall, about six and a half feet, and skinny to the point of emaciation. He wore a large hat with some sort of ornament or crest on it, and held a long crook in one hand. Before trooping back on to the bus, houses were visited by the driver to alert anyone interested, that the bus was about to leave. Two more people joined us, and we set off down the road, we had just travelled up.

The remainder of my visit to Gloucester was very ordinary. I had been before to its beautiful Cathedral, and so after some light refreshment, and having bought some foam rubber from the market, which I could hardly carry, I returned to the bus station. This time, the bus did not take a detour, and dropped me quite near to the entrance to the gate of the hotel. For some reason, I did not have my car keys, and was forced to enter the hotel with my burden, to find Sydney. The 'lads 'came to reception to view my return, and make joking comments, before my purchases were placed in the boot of the car. Little did they know, I had been in a shearing shed!

My aunt, who lived on the west side of Glasgow, had been urging me to visit, and with Ming in the back seat of the car, I set out to join the M8 at the roundabout close to the airport. At this point, the journey was interrupted by a flock of sheep, of all things. There was a delay, by which time, I decided not go directly to Glasgow. Instead, I followed the route to The Trossachs, ending up in Inveraray. There I found accommodation for the night, and next day visited the castle, home of The Duke of Argyll and climbed a nearby hill, with my lazy Chow Chow in tow. For once she became alert, bounding over the heather to raise grouse from their nesting places, and even attempting to catch them. From there, we did continue our journey to my aunt's house through beautiful scenery, and received her usual warm welcome.

Each evening, badgers followed the dyke at the side of the garden, across the road, and into the marley pits opposite. This took place just after dusk and was signalled by a few barks from Ming, if still in her outside kennel, as they passed. None was ever injured making the crossing there and back. No one could explain the reason for this ritual each evening, although they did sometimes overturn a rubbish bin and spread the contents on a lawn. The first thing our American student saw from her bedroom window was 'a strange animal' sitting on the middle of the roadway. Occasionally, a screech of brakes was heard at the time they would be making their crossing.

The garden flourished, with its annual bounty of fruit and vegetables. After ten years, the bramley was huge, the cordon apples producing well, as was the pear tree by the dining room door. The plum tree gave generously of its "golden eggs". In springtime, the dry stone dyke was a riot of colour under its line of tall poplar trees.

Sydney decided that some of the huge boulders, marking the base of the dyke, should be exposed, since it marked the boundary of what had been Mary Queen of Scots' land. All smaller stones and earth was removed and used to form a wishing well, where people could donate coins for outings for the children at Gogarburn. Poles and ropes were used to move the stones into better positions for viewing. Gurgling from the burn beneath, could be clearly heard, but water never came over the stones. The leylandii hedge was kept in place by constant pruning and did not exceed the ten inch width, I aimed for, well not often.

The year was nineteen eighty six. David was to be married in Bournemouth in the summer, and Sydney would retire later that year. Amongst our neighbours, only Bob and Kate would travel to Bournemouth for the wedding, Bob offering to drive the bride to church, as he did so often for local brides.

Sydney's brothers and brother-in-law, and my father were no longer with us, leaving their three elderly widows to make the journey on their own. The first stop was in Edinburgh to stay with us for a few days. Excitement grew, as hats and garments were unpacked and hung up in bedrooms. I was called forth to view three old women behaving like teenagers on the upstairs landing, changing suits, showing off hats, and even underwear. Kate was brought into the party, for tea, along with another neighbour, who my mother often visited independently when she was with us. Sydney's remark before his departure for the golf course was; "Are you sure the wedding's in Bournemouth?". Tina, David's aunt would be picked up by her daughter, Norma, to make more room for four of us on our journey south.

Before our departure, we were able to squeeze in a visit to Melville Castile, just outside Edinburgh where we had tea. Mother was able to see the castle she sang about, with her choir "Johnnie's gan' te Melville Castle, beets an'spur an' a'".

Sydney and I shared the drive south which was tedious, but uneventful. Once round Bristol, our final stop before Bournemouth was Warminster, which our passengers found attractive and quaint.

The hotel in Bournemouth, where the reception would be held was fully booked by a party of bowlers, so we housed ourselves in the hotel next door for two nights. June's family were quick to arrive to greet us. Bob and Kate arrived from Blackpool, where they had made a stop. There were just two days in which to enjoy the city, before the wedding. Gatherings grew in number, until all were assembled for the wedding to take place in Emmanuel Church, Southbourne. As with most

Scottish celebrations, this lasted a few days, with promises to meet in future.

The journey back to Edinburgh was again long and tedious. This time, we made a stop in Blackpool for only one night, where we were dragooned by an hotel manager, with rules of where to sit for breakfast, when to be seated and when to leave. As it happened, we arrived too late to be served with the evening meal, and had to search for an attractive place to eat. This was not the treat we had planned for the ladies. It was a relief, next day, to be approaching Moffat, an attractive border town, just off the M6, where we could relax and have a splendid meal. No sooner had we arrived home, than preparations had to be set in motion for celebrations with our neighbours, who had given so generously in their present to David. Friends from Gogarburn, too, had to be invited, but not until the following day when Kate would return. Mother and Ann, Sydney's sister, were both adept at serving food to many guests, and stepped in with gusto, making sandwiches, baking scones, pancakes and shortbread. Although nearing the end of September, the weather had been warm and sunny throughout the whole period of the celebrations, and continued so. To my relief, the party could be held in the garden. June had generously sent us home with the top tier of her wedding cake for the party, and her bouquet for the girls at Gogarburn. Pamela claimed the bouquet and went around school and hospital with a flimsy piece of cloth on her head curtsying to everyone she met. We wondered what she was thinking of herself, but very pleased in what she was doing.

Changes were in the air. Bob and Kate had bought a flat near to the Burgess golf course at Barnton, still in Edinburgh. It allowed for three garages, one for the Rolls, one for Kate's car and one for Bob's golf buggy, which he could drive up a short slope, across the road and enter the golf course in ten minutes. He had sold his dairy business, and bought a flat in Florida, again near to a golf course.

One neighbour had sold up for a more convenient house elsewhere in Edinburgh.

Our next door neighbour was contemplating a move, and two others were interested in the luxurious houses, now being built on floating foundations over the marley pits. Mr Gray had died, and two properties had been built in the field behind our garden, now that he could no longer enjoy the view of his beloved castle.

Sydney was due to retire in December, and farewell parties were on-going in the offices he visited throughout the year, with gifts of appreciation. His retirement from headquarters came almost as an anti-climax. He now had women in his audit section who presented him with a set of crystal glasses, with game birds etched on them, as a reminder to him that he had once said "no birds in this section, where officers are sent out to stay together". His gifts from the staff in general were a beautiful carriage clock, a golf trolley, and money to buy new clubs. I was invited to his retirement lunch, where the official photographer cut off our heads. I think he was trying to show off the beautiful bouquet which I had just been given. Speeches were delivered in his praise, and his response surprised me. It was memorable in that he rejected the figures given by The Treasury, as a possible percentage of profit expected from The Commission. Like any good Aberdonian, the wasteful proposals and unnecessary expenditure were firmly stated.

David had bought a house in Edgeware, London, and needed both Sydney and myself to help redecorate and set the garden to rights. I had already helped in his removal from West Hampstead, driving his little car, packed with boxes to Nolton Place. Its off-side door could be lifted off and its driving seat occasionally bounced back without warning, so I needed something firm behind me. Somehow, I felt at home in the south. Sydney did not care for walking on the Pentland hills, neither was he anxious to join The Burgess Golf Club, where Bob had put his name down years before. Mistakenly, I had relinquished my voluntary work at Gogarburn, thinking it would encroach on our new way of life. A period of boredom set in, and during a cold, soon to be foggy day, on the golf course, with hands frozen in the month of June, I realised I wanted to be back in Winchester. The decision was met with incredulity by my friends, but not by Sydney, who didn't seem to mind where we made our home, and didn't seem to harbour a wish to return to Aberdeen. How could we leave this dyke of colour, this garden, now so mature and productive! It was now that it dawned upon me that my joy was in creating a garden and watching it reach maturity, rather than keeping it after that stage. My urge was to change it drastically, as I had seen my father do when in a similar frame of mind.

Eleven

No barrier arose to selling our house. The market was buoyant, particularly, in the south, which was established when it was advertised for sale. Several properties attracted me in Winchester, two of which were within a stone's throw of Royal Winchester Golf Club, where we had played many times. Properties in this area were now selling at a spanking rate.

I was travelling by sleeper to view properties which were snapped up before my telephone call next day, showing an interest. Frustrated by this turn of events, Sydney and I decided that a new house in Chandlers Ford would suit us as a temporary solution. Some of 'The Young Wives' had moved to Alresford and South Wonston, but were still in touch. Our name went on the list for a soon-to-be built house on the new development at Valley Park, part of Chandlers Ford.

Two families showed keen interest in our property, one almost a company, with plans to build another house on the site at the end of the garden. This would not have suited the area, and we encouraged the other party, who also had plans for the site, but not building work. They had arrived from South Africa, where their bank had brought several employees back to Britain.

Although modest in their plans, they did include another garage, and the removal of the vegetable plot to accommodate an open-air swimming pool. I knew of no one in Edinburgh who had one of these without cover and a heating system. An offer was made to our solicitor and accepted, with a moving date of bonfire night, fifth of November nineteen ninety seven.

During that summer of waiting, a storm hit the south coast of England, devastating properties in Brighton, one of which had just been bought by the brother of a close friend and fellow dancer. Timidly, I rang our builder in Chandlers Ford, to ask if any of his half-built properties had been damaged. The reply came back, much to our relief, that only our back fence had been blown away.

Strangely, our builder's office was in the grounds of Cranbury Estate, home of the MacDonald Chamberlains, some far-off decedents of The Lords of The Isles, and from whom we would hold the freehold of our new property.

Time was running out as the end of August approached. This would be the last time we would have free access to the music and entertainment of The Festival and The Fringe. Like other tourists, it would be our lot to compete for accommodation in the hotels. I took away memories of a friendship with a young clarinettist from Los Angeles, of our times in The Gardens, watched and applauded as we danced to our favourite bands. Sydney's sense of humour came to the fore in our attendance at some of the comedy shows on The Fringe. Some of the more outrageous acts, caricaturing life in Scotland, he countered with his droll Aberdeen humour, joined sometimes by me, until one evening the cramped audience cheered him rather than the players.

A strange phenomenon was taking place in a field beyond our hedge. Each day, a number of young people were combing the ground. When asked about this, word came back that they were gathering mushrooms, common in fields where horses or cattle had been grazing. How enterprising some of us thought, because the era of natural food, and self-sufficiency was just beginning to dawn. Of course, their search was for "magic mushrooms" which contained an hallucinogenic substance used by drug users. This was graphically described to me listening to boys on the top of a bus. They could swim in oceans, float over mountains, and change into other people, and view themselves from afar.

At this time, too, our area was targeted by a gang of thieves, breaking into nearby homes. Eventually the culprits were tracked to Leeds. They used local 'Fagan's,' boys who could climb drain pipes or be thrown through a broken window. Ming was barking at a time after the badgers would have passed, so she was brought indoors. Isabel and Fred were visiting us when the shrill call of their alarm sounded. 'Och well,' said Isabel, 'Suppose it is our turn to-night,' and getting into one of her mink coats, led us towards their house. The thought of her beautiful lounge being ransacked, her paintings and porcelain being taken or broken, filled us with horror. A big extension had recently been completed at the back of the lounge to make a separate dining area or opened up as part of the lounge. This new wall, although mainly glass, did not afford easy access. It was plate glass, with a separate alarm. A break-in had been effected, through a broken window, its broken glass lying on the floor, and blood all over curtains and carpet. Isabel's sympathy went to the poor child who had been badly cut. The culprits were traced, and later charged.

It was a late autumn day, when I returned from shopping. Sydney had taken Ming to visit a friend. As I walked up the path, I noticed the side window open, and swinging on its hinges. Guessing that someone would be inside and had ignored my message on the back door no video, no camera, no money, I went to my neighbour, next door, and asked that she ring the police. I then took my number six from the garage, and holding it over the front doorway rang the bell, expecting someone to emerge and hopefully trip and land in the garden. After a reasonable delay,

I opened the front door to find our hall table smashed, along with a crystal vase. Sydney's gift from Rotary had gone, cigarettes were taken from a silver case but the case left. It smacked of young thieves. Most of our neighbours took precautions against burglaries; valuables were taped to the back of seldom used radiators, our cash in glasses cases. Ming was a good deterrent, being outside most of the time. The police found a list of houses with working alarms, or dogs marked on it. Bob's answer was a shotgun; when a boy climbed through his bathroom window, on the first floor. A gun faced the youngster in the bedroom which he entered, and he took refuge in a wardrobe, to be released when Bob heard the police arrive, with the caveat that he return to the ground by the same means he had gained entry. He was helped to the ground and taken away.

Parties were held at some houses to bid farewell, culminating in our final farewell dinner at The Ellersley Hotel on bonfire night; when we were showered with vouchers for plants and pots for our new garden.

Early next morning, we set off for Winchester, our household goods having been taken the previous day, to be stored in Southampton. At least, the journey was familiar, with snippets of memory, like the time I missed the M18, and when a journey in dense fog all the way from Stirling, ended in a lorry park where we had taken refuge, to find it almost deserted when we awoke around midday. The Merchant Navy Hotel in Southampton, now The Travel Lodge, would be our home for the next six weeks.

Walking round the docks, and visiting the Maritime Museum, near the ancient walls which had guarded the city over centuries from bombardment from the Solent, was a common start to the day. There still remained individual department stores where items tor the new house could be bought and selected. While choosing some crockery, I was lucky enough to meet a lady, whose accent exposed her ethnic origin. She was from Elgin, on the Moray coast. An immediate friendship sprang up, which still exists, and she became a dancer at Saint Francis, Valley Park.

Several meetings were held with our building contractor, all helpful and productive.

When I pooh-poohed the date given for completion, having seen a case on Harestock where one family brought their furniture from Inverness, only to find their dwelling half finished on the promised date, he became very serious, pointing out that his firm always fulfilled its obligation, leaving a couple of days leeway for a full inspection.

Our entry date was the twenty second of December, and that year, Christmas was a blur of activity and cold air. All windows had to be open to aid the drying out of newly plastered walls. The house was situated in a quite delightful close of nine houses, described by David as "yuppyland", since other owners were at least a decade younger than us. It would only be temporary, until we found a property in Winchester.

In a couple of months, we welcomed our baby granddaughter to stay, with her parents.

Southampton Airport was just a large shed, as far as passengers were concerned. It was owned by Mr De Savery, whose accountant lived in the close. She advised us that there were flights to and from Aberdeen, which suited my mother very well. Pick up and departures were uncontrolled, and made easy at the front entrance to reception. This would soon change when it was bought up to become the international airport, it is today, with new parking facilities and steep charges.

The house needed little attention. Our buyer in Edinburgh, wanted wooden floors throughout, which released our vast amount of top quality carpeting to be laid all over our new home, curtains fitted, or could be adapted to fit, so attention focused on the garden, which obviously had to be on two levels. Unlike Edinburgh, there were no stones of any size, only plenty flint.

Repairs were being carried out at Portsmouth Dockyard,

where Sydney, along with colleagues from The Treasury, had once carried out a work study. Left over stones were apparently waste, and a man still connected with the project, arranged for a load of the bigger stones to be delivered to our address. It came as a surprise to find a load of about thirty big stones in the driveway. Builders, still working on houses in the close, asked were we setting up in opposition. "Only at the back", came the reply, as we trailed and hauled the stones through the garage to the garden, this being the only route since the path at the side was of small pebbles.

Sydney began levelling the site by double digging, once again a huge task, better achieved by having loads of top soil brought in. This took many months, after which, the two parts could be divided in height by a rockery. As the borders were defined I was able to plant a James Grieve, which would be fertilised by one in our neighbour's garden. Evergreen bushes would hide the fences around the small area. The top area was made level first, with boards holding back the soil from falling into the lower area, so that grass could be sown there. Special plants were bought such as; a frementodendron [Californian Glory] and two clematis bearing names of people from whom we had received money or vouchers for our new garden; Kate, Gwen and Betty. A bottle brush plant represented Bob, as a reminder of his milk business. The top area was very stable, as a lawn grew, but we left the boards as reinforcement, until two layers of stones were laid. An obvious break in the soil suggested a place where steps could join the two levels. Our observers from the unfinished house in the close, brought a large piece of concrete, as a first step, and while artificial, it soon blended in with the others in rustic fashion.

It became clear, that the supply of stones was inadequate, "Mile Stones" in Eastleigh was able to make up most of the deficit, but only a couple could be transported at a time by car. Help was to come to our aid one evening, when attending a dance in Holy Trinity Church, hall, Winchester. Some repairs were being carried out to the structure of the church building, and piles of rubble sat at the edge of the pavement. Some stones were big enough for our purpose, so these were looked for and taken back in the car over a few weeks.

The rockery consisted of stones from Portsmouth harbour, Mile Stones, and Holy Trinity church, Winchester. In no time, it vied with the colourful dyke we had left in Edinburgh, with the added advantage that it faced the patio door from the sitting room to the garden.

The swing had been given away for the use of my niece and nephews, but I still needed a quiet neuk, for rest and contemplation, or just sitting in the sun. One corner was just the place, with a brick wall behind it, at the top of the garden. With some open trellis, Sydney built its surround, including an arched entrance - just right. By next season, clematis Montana was climbing into the leylandii trees of a neighbour, and japonicas adorned the trellis with their crop of quinces to make into jelly when ripened. The honeysuckle covering the arch had originated in Braemar, its root cuttings reaching all of our gardens in turn. This oasis of peace was of an irregular shape, not very suitable for being flagged.

A new material for paving patio areas was being advertised, it was called Belgo Quartz, and was made up of small stones in an attractive yellow/brown colour. This seemed ideal for the random shape of the area. When quoted, the price was far above what was expected, and I turned down the offer. A few days later, we were approached by the driver of the firm's lorry. He offered me enough material left over from a bigger job that had been completed that day, at an knock-down price if his passengers could lay it straightaway. Quite an elaborate surround had to be laid down before the material could be sealed with special glue. By the end of the afternoon, we had a hard standing at a price comparable with that of having it paved with flag stones. After the purchase of a white garden seat and flags laid in the grass to make a path to the entrance, the hide-away was complete.

The small area at the front of the house, carried a pink standard rose with annuals surrounding it, before a wide grass verge belonging to the council. The overhang along its front, called for a prolific climber. A blue wisteria was chosen, and although slow to grow at first it reached all the way along its track and along the garage overhang, threatening the garage overhang next door. Its blossoms cheered every passer-by in late spring; our then postman declaring it to be the best specimen in Hampshire.

The back garden was reached by a pathway on either side of the house, and required gates to ensure safety and privacy. By accident, when walking around a garden centre, I came upon a part selling ornamental pots and figures. It had a section for wrought iron pieces, where I found a gate which looked suitable for one of the paths. After checking its dimensions, and how it could be secured to the wall, I made the purchase, and was able to transport it home in the interior of the car. After several searches, and some weeks hence, I was lucky enough to find a similar gate, but shorter in height.

My welcome back to Winchester by the now dispersed wives group, was to be a meal in The Green Man, a pub, facing Southgate Street. Someone brought a sign, bearing the name of the group which had been adopted on my leaving for Edinburgh, "The Cruden Wives".

Only four members remained on Harestock, so our fortnightly meetings, which now took place in rotation in wives' houses, were to surrounding parts of the Winchester area; South Wonston, Chalk Ridge and Greenhill. The children had grown up and left home, by and large, and "young" had been dropped from our title, although the fun of big parties remained. Sydney showed no sign of developing any absorbing interests. He was not competitive at golf, and although urged to join The Woodland Trust, he had no wish to expand that further than his once a month Sunday's work in the ancient woods in Valley Park. There a few old men repaired pathways, cleared unwanted plants, and occasionally lit a bonfire of old branches. Over the years, the impact of their work was appreciated by walkers. People wanted to know where the huge badger set was, and where and when to look for our native daffodils. Butchers' broom was a favourite for children to use, its harsh leaves easily able to scour a piece of wood clean.

My mother did make it to Chandlers Ford, as did Sydney's sister. Both came separately on the tiny plane which we called the "Flying mini bus", soon to be taken over by K.L.M. It had thirty six seats, but looked after its passengers better than any other airline, with tea and coffee served on request in waiting rooms and every attention paid to in-flight comfort and information.

David, June and their baby daughter, Elaine, had moved from Edgeware to a large house in Horsel, Woking. It was easy for us to visit by car or by train, which we did often. Their garden was large and beautiful, but a challenge for anyone with little time to spare from daily work.

It was spring, and I felt in need of a relaxing holiday, not Aberdeen, a beach somewhere on the Mediterranean, perhaps, but Sydney wouldn't want that. I planned to go on my own, until he expressed his thought that if the destination was, say, Slovenia, he would accompany me. Knowing that two days on a beach would be the stretch of my relaxation, I agreed. Gardening books were laid aside for travel brochures and history books about this enchanting part of Europe. It was quite intriguing to be going almost behind the iron curtain, so recently raised. Our holiday was to be in Bled, on the edge of the beautiful lake of that name, and for a few days on the coast at Opatio. Excitement gripped passengers as the plane flew between a gap in the high mountains to make a landing a Ljubljana airport.

The tour guide was only available at the airport, where she bundled passengers into, or from coaches. This suited us quite well, since our questions had to be directed at local people. Sydney quickly learned that "duhan" was tobacco for his pipe.

The lady at the kiosk was able to tell us times that buses ran, if we could demonstrate our requests. Our waiter was anxious to learn English, and demanded that I look straight at him when replying. He was a tall fellow from Bosnia, asking a lot of questions, and finally taking us to a night club in Bled. There we learned some ethnic dancing, and were stupid enough to perform skip-change-of-step and pas de basque in our Scottish style, until we found ourselves alone on the dance floor being cheered. Each day was an adventure. We walked through the Vintgar, a narrow path by a river with steep cliffs on either side of the gorge. We spoke to farmers drying grain or straw on trellis-structures. One woman we met spoke amazing English. She was hanging up wet clothing for her eight children: no she did not have a job, "only farmer's wife".

Bojin beckoned, with its magnificent waterfall, and route towards the mighty Triglav mountain, with its summit very much covered in snow. I followed the path upward, until reminded that it was not our intention to climb, and returned to lower level.

The Plitviski caves were an added attraction. This time we were taken underground to a cathedral space where a unique pure white fish-like animal lived out its life without daylight.

Again I was asked to face a man. He was the driver of a bus which would take us far enough to view the Karawankee range of mountains. His terminus was KRNJSA - something I could not pronounce without vowels, like KRK, an island we were later to visit. I repeated his instructions, and everyone laughed People took us on foot, to where we would get the best view, and we trusted that the bus would return in two hours for the return journey.

One other place near Bled drew our attention. It was a small church in The Julian Alps, where Russian soldiers had been held prisoner by The Austrians. Some artefacts of their stay brought a feeling of unease. It was a sad place. Farther on, lay the Trenta Vailey, part of Italy. Here I was able to reach quite a height, while other passengers broke for lunch. The view of The Trenta and The Triglav, was of course, breath-taking. The steep cliff on the other side of the road, bore the iron footholds dug deep into the hillside by troops finding their way into Austria, during the wars of a previous century.

A coach arrived to take passengers to the second part of the stay in Slovenia. Most people we had seen at mealtimes, and were of mixed nationalities. Opatio, on the coast is a busy, cheerful town, with an Italian feel about it. Its hinterland is mountainous, and wooded; seaward is a cluster of islands sparkling in the Gulf of Fiume. The elusive tour guide did appear to tell us about the interesting hill town of Lovran, just to the north of Opatio. To the south, the town of Rijeka offered sailings to the islands but was a dull town, we thought, with grey buildings, and poor shopping. Its activity concentrated around the harbour area. A bus took us along the the coast road, to where we were able to follow a rough path to the hill fort of Lovran, hundreds of feet above us. Ancient stone walls surrounded the fort, but inside, nothing seemed to be missing from that of a small village. Cafe's and shops displayed their work-a-day goods. There even was a small market, with a section devoted to souvenirs for visitors. We ate, and enjoyed the views, before descending, at almost running pace, to wait for a bus to come along and take us back to Opatio.

The tour guide appeared once more in our hotel to ask would we be willing to comment on newly designed clothes, being displayed in a cultural centre in the city. There would be no payment, but food and drinks afterwards. Naturally, I jumped at this opportunity. Sydney was not quite sure.

We were to be collected next morning by horse-driven carriage, and driven through the town, advertising the display. We felt like royalty and acknowledged people's greetings as we passed. Our horseman had good English, and attempted to tell us why so many houses remained unfinished. The state, at one time, had owned all the properties, but now it seemed people were allowed to purchase their houses floor by floor or add a floor.

The tour guide was there as we were helped down from the carriage, and taken upstairs to a quite dark room. Here, it was explained to us, that the clothes would be displayed by a mannequin, and I, in particular, would comment on them as they were put on film. This, I thought went well. The clothes were imaginative, but not vulgar, so I ventured much genuine praise. The frock with O.P.A.T.I.O. woven into a side panel was most attractive.

At the end of the parade, we were taken downstairs for Turkish coffee, little buns and much talk, none of which was understood by us. We became of interest, when we were discovered to be Scots and not English, used to high mountains and snow every winter. Ice bunkers were discussed; holes dug in the ground where ice could be stored in winter for use in the summer. Kindrochit, and the other lodges in Braemar had those. We were invited upstairs again, to be asked would we repeat the process. Lighting, or something related, was not entirely to the satisfaction of the cameraman. Nothing was to change as far as we were concerned. I tried very hard to convey my delight and enthusiasm on seeing the garments for the first time, but this was hard. I did ask for two items to be shown again, and delivered some different comments. All was deemed perfect, and the filming would be sent to Europe and America to be shown in their world-class stores. After enjoying a 'Middle Eastern' lunch, we were driven back to the hotel by the same horseman.

On the last evening of our stay, the man who we spoke to most days in his garden, invited us in his broken English to a party in the evening. "Dober Dan", one amongst two or three phrases, we knew, opened many doors for us. This might well have been a late night with many toasts, so, with an early start next day, we shook our heads, and reluctantly declined.

The flight back was from Ljubljana, and uneventful. I

applauded Sydney on his mention of Slovenia as a destination, and, although never could it be termed relaxing, I returned refreshed, and with a store of memories of this unique part of Europe.

Settlement in Chandlers Ford, meant life divided between Winchester, Southampton, and Romsey, all within a few miles of home. Several department stores had closed during our absence from the area, and now large housing estates reached into the countryside, including Valley Park. Here, there were few facilities. A school had been completed and opened, but church and community and health centres still were missing.

Along the road leading to North Baddesley stood a tiny church, going back centuries, reputedly with a priest hole and secret passage running below the road to the house on the opposite side. It had a valuable painting unknown to the congregation, which was stolen soon after our arrival, causing much comment in the local press and bringing visitors to the church.

Services were not conducted there every Sunday, but I was able to cycle the short distance to the church when appropriate. Saint Francis, Valley Park opened its door for worship some months later. The organ in the little church was upstairs, and it took the elderly organist some time to climb the rickety stairs to reach it. Apart from the whooshing around of incense, it could have been a service held in Scotland. There were two psalms, and three hymns announced on the board. Children sat at the front, and were addressed with a bible story, before being dismissed to sit with their parents, or draw pictures at the back of the church.

The opening of Saint Francis Church, and removal from its temporary site at Mulberry Corner, was a landmark for the housing estate. Along with the school and its shared hall, it brought people together, young and old. Although, Church of England, Saint Francis was part of an ecumenical venture with The Methodist Church and The United Free Church, both in Chandlers Ford. It attracted families from different religious backgrounds. The vicar was young and active, making it his business to get to know his flock, and get his church off to a good start. We knew that we would be happy in this community, just struggling to its feet.

Roads had to be realigned to take the increased volume of traffic. With woodland to the east, and open fields on the right, it seemed incongruous to be erecting traffic lights, but this proved a necessity, as more and more vehicles used the road.

At the foot of the hill to the south of our house, the flood plain became obvious after rain storms. The small stream to the east of the area did not cope well with heavy rain, overflowing its banks and footpath, and flooding an area where houses were intended to be built. To the west two ponds fed into the stream adding to the flood risk. The council wisely decided that the ponds be extended to hold more water, in particular the water from many springs which fed into them. These ponds were to be known as "balancing ponds " and relieved flooding farther downstream. They were soon to be popular to walk around, and attracted wild life and birds. A heron landed on one quite regularly, his patient eye focused on any movement in the water.

Gradually, a feeling of cohesion emerged. A centre now existed of; school, church and pub on one side of the road, with; parking areas, health centre, community centre, general store, hairdresser alongside a fish and chip cafe' on the other.

After a long wait for the southernmost residents, all daily needs could be catered for, except, perhaps a postal service.

I decided that a bicycle would be an advantage to me in such a place, and seeing an advert for an old Raleigh, I became its owner. It would replace the one I had been given in Edinburgh, which had small wheels, and gave little reward for all the effort of pedalling. The centre could be reached in next to no time, and make it home, cycling uphill, in ten minutes. Along to the Post Office at Hitingbury, was made quick and easy.

Twelve

Our welcome back into The Waverley Dance Club, had been met with enthusiasm and affection. At the first opportunity, I was offered the job of secretary. This was not an arduous task; just booking halls for dances when dancers from clubs far and wide would require tickets to be sent out with relevant information. Dancers liked advance knowledge of displays being arranged; when men would appear in kilts, and ladies in white dresses and tartan sash, pinned at the shoulder with a suitable brooch. It was mainly spreading information, and dealing with regular events.

On one occasion, the fiddlers turned up with the wrong tune for a complicated dance. The team was to perform on The High Street, where traffic had been halted just by The Butter Cross. In the confusion, some dancers started the dance which was being played, while others set off on the one planned. Jock was pulling his reluctant partner round in the middle, when someone had the sense to call "Stop". Viewers cheered, thinking the display to be over, and moved away, while we regrouped and gave the performance expected.

After some years as secretary, two ladies, who had been accompanying us to "Waverley", were joined by a young oceanographer and his wife, also living in Chandlers Ford. The suggestion was put to me that a class be started in Saint Francis Church.

Without much hope of attracting many people, I prepared a presentation, with background to Scottish Country Dancing, its introduction by Mary Queen of Scots as a feature of the ballroom, and therefore its use of French terms for some movements.

About fifteen people from church attended the meeting, and were anxious to try this new activity. At this point there was still very little of a recreational nature.

In church our space was limited. Sydney said his contribution to the venture would be the purchase of records, later to be CDs, all to come from Highlander Music, a firm in Muir of Ord, north of Inverness. Steps and simple formations were struggled through at first, but at each session more people attended, to be helped by those used to fast music and quick turns. The church, itself, could be used, but something in my background refused this concession, except for temporary use, when a row of dancers could skip round without constraint.

A fee of three pounds was suggested, with any profit going to the church and charities.

By April, dancing had moved to the school, cum church hall, with ample space, and a kitchen for our use. Numbers had grown to over thirty dancers. Four men had sent to Edinburgh to purchase kilts. The club was truly launched.

I resigned my commitment as "Waverley's" secretary, but Sydney and I continued to attend the club each week. Friends from South Wonston, introduced us to a colonel and his wife, returning from military duties in Brunei, where they had learned some Scottish dances, and were keen to continue this pastime. After a short time dancing at "Waverley", they too decided to start a class for this at Worthy Down, the home of the military, just north of Winchester. By autumn, there was talk of us having an invitation dance at Saint Francis. The hall was booked for a Saturday evening, and invitations circulated to surrounding clubs. Worthy Down came forward with sixteen names and "Waverley" with thirty.

Eighty was the maximum number, and that was soon reached. A supper of savouries and exotic puddings was expected at these events. A big shop at Asda, had to be made by me and a helper on the day of the dance. Exotic cheeses and items for salads, after eights to accompany tea and coffee were on the list. Puddings were brought by dancers who excelled in this field, so much so, that our dance in Saint Francis hall became known as "The Pudding Dance". Each person was expected to bring two plates, cutlery and a wine glass, to be taken home washed or unwashed as people wished. It made clearing up easier. Except for a few, we all brought our "kit ". A church member set up the music for us, making sure it came over as we wished, and that I could use the microphone from the best position.

In spite of a modest charge, a substantial profit was made, so that over the years, thousands of pounds, were donated to church, school and local charities. Because of the generosity of church and school, the fee for the evening was reduced to one pound fifty per dancer, still making a good profit. It was recognised that an activity, bringing together all ages and sexes, for fun, fitness and friendship, was of benefit and to be encouraged.

The club at Worthy Down, established by the colonel, thrived and reciprocated with splendid dinner/dances, and a Burns Supper every year. Poems were delivered and funny translations made of "The Address to The Haggis.' ' A Toast tae the Lassies' was a flight of the imagination, each time. At a check point, cars were stopped before continuing towards the dining room, it still being the time of I.R.A. bombings. This continued for some time after the threat, and on one occasion, recognising the sentry we spoke our names and were waved ahead. A comedian in the backseat, grabbed the sentry's arm, saying "You've missed Gerry Adams, he's in the boot". For several seconds, it seemed touch and go, if we would be allowed to proceed. A ritual had been established that Sydney's first act on reaching the dining room bar, was to place a glass of 'malt' in the hand of our host, Peter.

A big disappointment awaited us upon our return to Hampshire. The Salisbury club had shrunk in numbers, since our departure to Edinburgh. Their dances in the town hall had been events of grandeur during our previous stay, and it was hard to accept the change.

In Saint Francis, some girls were allowed to attend the first part of our class. All were adept at picking up steps and formations, helping, and sometimes demonstrating to older dancers. As in Edinburgh, it gave them great confidence to act in other ways, knowing that they could do things better than some of their seniors. It was natural for these girls to accompany us to dances in Bournemouth, Chichester or Winchester, when accompanied by a parent or trusted adult, making a safe introduction to the adult world they would soon be joining.

One dancing couple, were keen long-distance walkers and cyclists. They were noted for "head down and reach the goal", without much regard of terrain or landscape. Both had bikes with dropped handlebars, and sped along at a very fast rate. A modest bike ride was to Stockbridge via Romsey, and return through Winchester.

A group of dancers were going to dance in the open air at Loseley House, near Guildford.

Lifts were arranged, but the two cyclists said they would get there under their own steam, which in their case was true. Soon after the rest of us had parked, they appeared on their bikes. We thought they would be visiting in the area, but this was not the case, neither were they to cycle home. After an afternoon dancing, they mounted their cycles to cycle to High Wykham, where their daughter lived. A people-mover, owned by one of our friends, who enjoyed a glass of wine at a supper / dance, was licenced for a young dancer just left university, to drive. She only drank water or tea. Most of us were glad to go by this means, to out-lying halls, near Chichester and the New Forest, where parking could be a difficulty. For Sydney and myself, our range was from Corfe Mullen and Bristol in the south and west, to Brighton, and Windsor in the east and north. It was normal to attend a dance somewhere every Saturday night, travelling through sleet and rain in winter, and sunny landscapes in summer.

As the millennium approached, celebrations were under discussion. Most of our club were going to be able to attend, along with some long-standing friends from nearby clubs, and a few non-dancers, who had to be accommodated. The programme was left for me to compose, and I did not want it just to follow the pattern of an ordinary dance. An idea formed that the entertainment be divided into decades, according to dancing and music popular during each time, throughout the century. Ten separate groups formed to dress according to the decade chosen, and produce an appropriate dance, in secret from the others, so that we could all enjoy surprises. This proved extremely popular. Most people made their own costumes, but some went as far as to hire outfits. A memorable one was of a lady dressed as a nineteen 20's flapper, when we all attempted a Charleston. Of course, in lines across the hall we danced "The Palaise Glide". More modern attempts came in thigh boots, borrowed from a niece, when we danced to music from the seventies. And so the evening progressed, interspersed with a few Scottish Country dances, until supper time. This had to be an exotic relay of savouries and puddings of the century, found in old recipe books, borrowed in one instance from the local library.

During the day, the men, taking the initiative, had decorated the hall and hung a huge net from the ceiling, where one hundred red balloons were placed, when blown up, to be released on the stroke of midnight, on this very special Hogmanay Night, it would be the start of the twenties.

All remnants of supper had to be washed and cleared away, and equipment packed into the boots of cars. Only sparkling glasses and a decanter of malt whisky remained on a small table in the corner. The keenest dancers had been invited to arrive half an hour before the others, so that they would have a few favourite dances before the full programme began. Now, the programme consisted of Scottish Country dances, with only one concession for those who were not able to join in.

Excitement was building, as minutes ticked by. Watches were glanced at, and the hall clock checked for accuracy. The time had almost come; not only a new year, but a new century. We gathered round, as we always did, waiting for the moment of change over to arrive. A whistle sounded from the pub next door, and our clock stood at midnight. The dancer who had shinned up his ladder to put up the netted balloons, now pulled a string, and they fluttered down upon us. With the press of a button, music accompanied our singing of Auld Lang Syne. Greetings were exchanged all around the hall, and drams of whisky celebrated the new millennium.

Fireworks, shot from the pub garden, illuminated the dark sky, and we were able to stand outside and enjoy the spectacle. Faintly, the sound of ship's hooters reached our ears. A great gladness swept over the company, as we made our way home.

The school was burying a capsule of life there at the time, and I was invited to contribute our involvement in the celebrations. I wrote a piece about the evening, along with a programme of dances, what we ate and how we dressed, tied up with a tartan ribbon round it, to go underground and be read in fifty years' time.

As years progressed and dancers formed close friendships, a suggestion was put forward that we filled the mini bus and set off for Edinburgh. Plans were made about who would take turns of driving the vehicle, and what stops, if any, would be made. Insurance cover settled and bookings made in an hotel, just off The Royal Mile, we were ready to be on our way.

A box had been attached to the back of the vehicle to carry

luggage. Kilts, and other parts of highland dress took up a lot of room, and the attachment proved a great asset. There would be no stops overnight, only stops for food and to meet with a couple, who had chosen to make the journey in their own car. After an early start, the M6 was reached just before the morning rush hour. The weather was fine and the chatter loud, as we swept northwards. Just after lunch, we left the motorway for the route through the border town of Moffat, the Pentlands coming nearer as we travelled. A few passengers had visited Scotland before, and some only by train. It was Sydney's and my opportunity to point out the many interesting features of the countryside, including Penicuik, where the Edinburgh Crystal factory was open for sales and the charming Roslin Chapel which we would later visit. Late afternoon traffic was heavy and our progress to the hotel slow. Sydney took the wheel for this part of the journey and delivered us safely to our hotel.

There was to be dancing in The Gardens, that evening, so after showers and an early meal, and men dressed in kilts, we lined up with other dancers. Sydney and I were immediately recognised, and introduced those dancers to our friends from the south. Invitations for drinks afterwards were turned down. We were all tired out. Next day we did not sally forth as a group. It had been decided that our interests varied, and that we would "do our own thing". Two things we did attempt as a group was the climbing of Arthurs Seat, and a visit to The Royal Yacht, moored at Leith Docks. One member of our dance troop had at one time been an engineer on The Q.E.2, and spent his time in the engine room, while others of our party enjoyed the furnishings and comfort of this small vessel, which spoke of escape for the Royal family, and adventures around the islands of our west coast.

This dancer had also served time on The Shieldhall, a vessel moored in the Solent to collect refuse from the waters. When interviewed on radio, about his contrasting services. "Aye" he replied I went from the affluent to the effluent".

Each morning, we were able to listen to the exploits of others, how they got lost, getting to The Museum of Antiquities in Queen Street and of the bargains picked up in major stores.

Back, in the south, the group was recounting episodes of the holiday in Edinburgh; Mary King Close, just off The Royal Mile, which had been blocked up during an outbreak of the plague and was a capsule of the time when it functioned as a shopping lane, of Mary Queen of Scots, bathhouse, outside Holyrood Palace, where she went twice a year, it is said, to bathe. Who needs a shower every day, or even once a week! Eventually, all aspects of the holiday were exposed and laughed about, often, brought to mind by the name of a dance.

Contact with The Forestry Commission was not severed when we were able to attend meetings of The F.C. Retirement Association, held in Queen's House, Lyndhurst, in the New Forest. This ancient building housed the local office of the New Forest area and was the centre for our excursions into remote parts of the forest for a picnic, and lecture on plants or animals. It was sheer bliss to be accompanied by a local dweller, who knew the secrets of where the usual animals, and sometimes the not so usual, would be hiding.

In spite of the many dance holidays in Britain, Sydney never wanted to join those going farther afield into Europe. I, on the other hand, jumped at the opportunity of visiting Cyprus, and the mid-European cities; Prague, Vienna, and Budapest.

Something seemed to be lacking in our lives. It was the daily routine of set hours, and meeting with people, which a round of golf did not quite fulfil. In passing one day, I caught sight of an advertisement in the window of the local stationers for an assistant. Without any hope of success, I applied for the job, temporary, with short hours. My thoughts, when I reached home were that Sydney would think "if she can apply for a job locally, then I could do something outside the home, too". Weeks passed without reaction.

For me, the work was interesting and varied to a point, customers habits were learned, and conversations covered more than just the weather, as we became more familiar. The old Raleigh bike with basket on the front took me back and forth to my work each day. The hours were fixed so that the lunch break did not attract remuneration. When my payment was added to my husband's retirement pension, and taxed, the amount left was a mere pittance.

The arrival of a second grandchild at Woking, and the need for my attendance there, put an end to my working life in Chandlers Ford. The gesture had failed completely, in finding a regular interest to fill his hours, but I had made many friends, in particular a couple living in our close, who came regularly for a newspaper. Joyce was Cornish with a large family living there. Her husband was, like Sydney, a retired civil servant, having been employed by the then Ministry of Works, as an architect. Together, we joined The Civil Service Retirement Association which met in a hall near Saint Boneface church in Hursley Road.

For a time, our sedate pattern of life was broken only by the visits of our grandchildren to stay by themselves from a remarkably early age. Both Sydney and I felt it the greatest privilege that their mother, in particular, put so much trust in our care of each when they arrived for their "turn". It was then, that our bonds with each was cemented and that the other could have full attention of his or her parents. "Pooh bridge" was an attraction. It spanned the stream running to the east of the estate, next to the local railway line. Leaves and sticks could be thrown over and watched as they floated away, or were caught on the edge of the bank. There were walks through the ancient woodlands, searches for Mr Brock, around his huge mound, where holes led to the homes of baby badgers and a vast grassy area for games. Yuppyland had every amenity for happy living.

Our contentment was shattered one evening when Sydney and I were preparing to go to a dance at Basingstoke. He felt sick and was gripped by a severe pain in his chest. The doctor was called, and advised he be taken right away to hospital in Winchester, where someone would await his arrival. He did not require medical intervention on this occasion, and was sent home within a week. Friends had insisted on taking me to dance in Winchester during the week, and as we passed Sydney's window, like children we all waved and called "goodnight".

The respite lasted several years, until I became aware of similar symptoms arising once again. After several visits to the local health centre, a diagnosis was made by a friend who was a midwife, that Sydney had a severe heart problem. My pursuit of an official diagnosis was swift and effective. After a few tests at Southampton General, it was proposed that he be put on a list for bypass surgery at Midhurst Hospital, once a hospital for servicemen, but now used by McMillan Cancer, and other special needs, where a helicopter brought patients to a surgical unit.

Sydney's operation was scheduled for the first of April, which amused us. The patient had to present himself two days before that date. This gave me time to assess the time of the journey between Chandlers Ford and the hospital near Midhurst. My intention was that I would visit each day. On the appointed day, I met with the surgeon and doctor, who explained the procedures about to take place, and the risks involved.

The beauty of the turn of the century building, with its solid oak staircase and wide corridors, calmed me as I entered for this strange and unknown, experience of medical science about to be performed on my husband. Sydney was to occupy a room by himself, with personal en suite facilities, just like any good hotel. As always, he was cheerful, listening to the course of events and outcomes [only small errors or happenings upset him, big events, he took in his stride, as now]. A farewell kiss, and I was left alone, and he to face the trauma ahead.

The hospital had accommodation for visitors to stay overnight, so I did not have to seek out an hotel in nearby Midhurst. The grounds were attractive, with seats near to borders of spring flowers, which would soon be a riot of colour, wallflowers and tulips. I was to remain for three nights, and have my food with Sydney when that became possible. Mostly, I ate in the restaurant where staff gathered. Surgeons and doctors came to know why I was there, and would come over to comment on Sydney's progress.

The first night, I was invited to stand by his bed in "intensive care", holding him firmly from any movement. Morning came, and I had no recognition of the hours I had spent just standing there. Gradually, it appeared that the procedure had been a success, and that I could start coming each day. After my journey, from Chandlers Ford, it was most kind to have a cup of coffee brought to me by one of the staff. The whole complex was well summed up by a Dutch doctor one day, when I was thanking him for his concern and interest. Well, this is the mansion, and that is the "factory" meaning Southampton. It is true that a busy general hospital could not have operated on a similar level.

Within a week, Sydney was recovering from his corpse-like state. He was walking round the room, and peering out of the window at the helicopter, which took off or landed most days. Our walks along the corridor, with seats at suitable intervals, lengthened each day until we could venture out into the garden.

The weather was fine, and only once was my journey home, slow and frustrating.

The rain was heavy, and upon joining the A272, two lorries were in front of me. To have overtaken one would have been a feat, two, impossible. Upward, through Steep, I followed, a line of impatient drivers joining the queue. After two weeks, David, June and the grandchildren were able to visit, which was a great encouragement for Sydney and myself. Later two of our friends expressed a wish to see Sydney, and release me from my daily journey. They were welcomed in the same cordial way as I was, and could only admire the running of this splendid hospital. Part of it was given over to McMillan Cancer Care, and someone I had met once was receiving treatment there, so I was able to surprise him with a visit one afternoon. Sydney was released after four weeks, having had the extraordinary number of five stents to support his heart. Recovery was swift, and soon we were hosting "a recovery dance", in Valley Park.

Normality had returned, and the year filled up with local dances, holidays to the Crieff Hydro, in Scotland, where in daytime we roamed the hills of Perthshire, or visited our friends in Edinburgh. Once, Bob and Kate were staying at Gleneagles hotel, where we were well fed and joined them for a round of golf.

The north of England featured in some of our dance adventures, Hawkshead being the favourite place to stop. The proprietor of one of the hotels was himself a Scottish dancer, and to this end, had the floor in his dining room ripped up and replaced with a wooden one, so that tables could be cleared away and the dance begin.

Again, daytime took us into beautiful countryside, charming villages like Grassington, and to Grizedale Forest, where Sydney could meet people who knew him from The Forestry Commission.

The west country was not forgotten, Cheltenham was on the list, and on our way there we could visit Prinknash Abbey, founded by monks in the tenth century, later rebuilt in the twelfth, and again by its monks in this century. The brother of one of Sydney's colleagues had been a monk at the Abbey, and was well remembered by those with whom we toured the building, and its grounds. Peace was upon us as we resumed our journey to Cheltenham.

On the final evening of our stay, Sydney took seriously ill, and had to be taken to hospital by ambulance, with me following behind. It was dusk, and of course, I got lost for part of the way.

This time, I was forced to find accommodation as near as possible to the hospital.

The company with whom we had booked this dancing holiday, were most helpful and concerned that I be looked after. I was invited to dine with them before returning to the hospital. This time, Sydney was not in 'intensive care', but it would be best to have someone by his bedside. For a second time, I was to stand sentinel over him all through the night.

Having checked his records, the decision came that he would stay in hospital for four days, and any further action would be in Winchester. I stayed in Cheltenham for three nights, but travelled to and from from home for the remaining two nights. Clothes had to be washed and changed, along with other necessities brought.

All my time was not spent in the hospital. There was a book fair in town which I visited, and some shopping to buy a new raincoat. The weather had taken a turn for the worse. On the day of release, paperwork continued until well after lunch, the wait was not easy to bear. Each time a conclusion was reached, another snag appeared. By four o'clock, we were on our way, along the M4 motorway, this time, in case help had to be signalled. With much relief, we arrived home, and Sydney was tucked up in a bed in the dining room downstairs. First thing in the morning, our doctor called. He said nothing as I opened the door, just gave me a hug and stepped into the dining room, as I indicated.

Arrangements were made that day for Sydney's admission to The Royal Hampshire hospital. Upon arrival, the waiting doctor had notes in his hand, saying to Sydney "if this had happened on the golf course, -- no chance, but we'll see you to rights". I was banished to a waiting room and after some time two men passed, one jingling keys, and I knew drastic treatment was imminent. This being confirmed, I made my way home, forcing my mind to the conclusion that all would be well.

David arrived in support, in spite of his third child having just been delivered in hospital. The visit cheered us both. The operation was successful. All was well.

After ten years, a letter was sent to Southampton expressing our gratitude for the many years of active life afforded to Sydney from the intricate work performed at Midhurst, and Winchester.

Thirteen

By twenty eleven, Sydney had failed in health. Several ischemic incidents, from which he quickly recovered, had slowed him down somewhat. My eightieth birthday was to be celebrated with a dinner/dance in Saint Francis church hall. A lift was arranged for Sydney before starting time, so that he could welcome guests coming from Bournemouth, Southsea, and clubs around the area. Eventually, he appeared in time, having sent his "lift " away and having taken an hour to get into kilt, socks, and full highland dress, after which he walked all the way down Knightwood Road to the hall; sheer determination had ruled his actions. A glass of whisky was demanded on arrival. Much was made of his feat, and he happily circled the tables greeting the ten people now seated. A family member was allocated to each of the eight tables.

There was a strange occurrence connected with the company, I employed to provide the meal. I chose this company from an advert in the local magazine for Chandlers Ford, and was delighted with their food and service. The proprietor mentioned earlier, that he had done a lot of catering for big parties on their yachts, going from The Solent. Straight after the meal, he wanted payment which I was happy to provide. Two nice pieces of cutlery were left behind, so next day, I thought to return these to the address I had been given in Valley Park, only to discover there was no such place. The advert never appeared again, and the telephone number, I had been given was never answered.

This was the last big event Sydney was able to enjoy. Because speech had deteriorated, he was receiving speech therapy from a charming Irish lady at Brendon Care, a complex on Knightwood Road. She introduced him to some of her students, who appreciated a bit of light banter. One morning we waited. When her door opened, Sydney countered with his stick, shaking it vigorously, and pointing it at her. His actions proved too much, and he slipped first on to an armchair, and then to the floor. Everyone waiting, laughed and helped him to a sitting position. Neither I nor the speech therapist thought any serious hurt could have occurred. A "Brendon Care" assistant arrived on hearing the laughter, insisting that an ambulance be sent for, in case a finger of negligence be pointed at any of the staff.

The A&E department at "The Royal Hants" was busy, even in late afternoon, so we had to wait at each barrier, before reaching the X ray unit. An X ray revealed a suspected break in the pelvis, and further tests were to confirm this. The stark choice, between allowing the repair to heal on its own, and not be able to walk, or have an operation, which offered a better outcome, was left with us until the following day.

Separately, we agreed that the bones be set. Sydney, always teasing and positive, thinking if this course "finished him off" then it was a better alternative than never walking again.

I knew how miserable he would be restricted in that way. The operation to set the bones would go ahead. Unfortunately, his health was not good enough for his body to cope with the procedures necessary. In spite of excellent treatment, and sympathetic care, he gradually declined over a week. Many friends visited, and all the family had seen him, expecting a slow return to normal health. The second of August was our son, David's birthday, and Sydney had forbidden him to visit that day, since he had seen him two days, previously. Instinctively, I knew that the situation was terminal, hoping for just another day. The fourth of August would be our granddaughter's birthday, and | had brought a card for Sydney to scrawl something on it.

On the third of August, I made my visit as usual, having baked some pancakes for the 'girls' as he had instructed. The doctors were late in their round that day, and although speech had gone from Sydney, his face lit up, as he pointed to his watch and indicated disapproval.

My neighbours were wont to call when I returned from my hospital visit, but that evening I was alone for tea, and quite relaxed, when the telephone rang to tell me that Sydney had died, and that I could come at any time to the hospital. Immediately, I called David, who was strolling with his wife along the riverside at Surbiton. Against my protests that I was alright, he replied that he would arrive that evening, and together, we would say our "farewells". Everyone experiencing this trauma, realises the loneliness of losing a loved one. Although expected, when the blow falls, it's never prepared for. My heart went out to the young doctor, who met with me the following day to explain the circumstances of the death. How can this be easy for such a young person to have to convey this report to anyone. He did it with the utmost care and sympathy, and I thanked him for his efforts at kindness and consideration. In return, he thanked me for being philosophical, and not weeping. It was a time to keep emotions private; there being no need to express grief to complete strangers.

It was with much gratitude, that I received the sympathy and support brought to me by neighbours, church members, friends and dancers.

The funeral took place at Saint Francis Church. I had booked the hall and caterers for a drink and afternoon tea [sherry for the ladies, and whisky for the men], Sydney had always stipulated. The sun shone. A marquee had been erected in the garden of the church, so everyone was able to circulate and have tea out of doors. Our vicar was on sabbatical leave and so precluded from taking the service, but our minister and friend from The Methodist Church, Peter, took his place, while 'our' Peter and his wife joined the congregation.

The coffin was brought into church to the accompaniment of "Nimrod", suitable music for one brought up in Aberdeen, with so many attachments to the sea. Our granddaughter read the lesson, David spoke, as did I, but only shortly as I feared a break in my voice when expressing my admiration for Sydney's acceptance and good humour throughout his many traumas. He was taken out to the sound of a favourite Strathspey tune, 'The silver tassie'. After a short service at Southampton Crematorium, the family returned to their friends in the garden. His ashes lie, some in Duthie Park, Aberdeen, and at the top of Saint Catherine's Hill here in Winchester, where we loved to walk during our first stay in the city, so many years ago.

During the previous year, I thought that we should move to a house near to the centre of Romsey or Winchester, where Sydney could walk to fetch his newspaper, and meet other customers. He did not like the idea of a move, and the many properties viewed, proved quite unsuitable, mainly up-hill in Winchester, or with steps up to the front door. In Romsey, I viewed narrow conversions and properties too near to water to be safe from flooding. Our house had been on the market since early summer, with potential buyers making offers. It was taken off the market during Sydney's time in hospital, and until after the funeral.

The situation had changed, but I still considered a move to Winchester to be attractive, after all, it was where we had intended to live all along. Bus, train and road connections were excellent for the family, now living in Surbiton, some seventy miles from Winchester. It also offered easy access to London,

Waterloo, and to Southampton Airport, just across the road from Parkway Station.

No likely property was overlooked. Houses at Badger Farm and Harestock were viewed, but it became obvious the even a flat without a garden would prove more convenient in the long run. An insight into accommodation can be revealing to oneself.

A flat in the centre of Winchester was rejected because, it lacked a window from its small kitchen area, adjoining a large living area. The small excluder fan would never have coped with smells coming from my daily cooking and baking. All the time, I was drawn back to Saint Cross, with its memories of walks by the river, and David's fishing rod trailing in the water, hopeful of a bite from a trout; the daily run to the top of Saint Catherine's Hill, with Rex. It was approaching decision time. I had looked at two flats in Saint Cross, which were attractive and suitable, when David spotted an advertisement for one in "The Normans", the block in which we had lived almost fifty years before, while waiting for our house in Winchester to be completed. Although, marginally different in layout, from the one we had first occupied, most features were the same. More garages had been added to the site, with one allocated to each flat, and mostly used by the owners for storage, rather than made available to tenants, thus reducing the need for open parking in what could be an attractive entrance. The garden area nearest the parking area, had obviously not been tended for many years, and the shrubs in front of the building exceeded their life span by decades. The garden at the back of the building retained its attraction with its trees and expanse of grass, and two wooden seats. What was left of careful planting, added a bit of colour from time to time. A clematis, planted by the lady selling the flat, became a welcome sight of purple climbing into the trees in the spring. Otherwise, the area was a mess. Rubbish had been thrown at the back of the borders, a plant in an urn had died, and grass was poorly nurtured, but cut at regular intervals. The gardening club, with its equipment stored at the back of the "bin store" had long given up. No borders were tended, no pruning of trees took place, and one seat was legless. Owner-occupiers had been, to a large extent, replaced by tenants, bringing cash to owners with scant interest in outside maintenance or convenience. It was a big step down for this typical building of the nineteen sixties, and an on-going disappointment to me, when I conjure up what it once was. A conversation about which plants would grow best is so unlikely now, Miss Rafferty, interested and informed, was full of ideas. David knew to raise his cap to her in passing. In spite of this there remained little doubt in my mind that this was where I 'wanted to live'. A viewing of the flat, almost opposite the one I had previously occupied, was arranged with a local estate agent.

I had forgotten the large expanse of hallway in two of the four hallways at their entrances, and was suitably impressed to find this. No decorations adorned the walls, and no large table sat opposite the doorway, with its bowl of flowers lighting up the rather dark area. Only a functional grey board was placed near the entrance, displaying rules and regulations about fire and rubbish collections, all of which had been received individually by residents, and most likely never read. Who in the face of a fire alert, would wish to nip downstairs to read the notices. Thick black tiles with flecks of red and white covered the floor and stairway, and without relief, gave out the feeling of municipal office, rather than entry to homes.

The flat for sale was on the first floor, with the sitting room facing east towards a row of high trees; a large beech and evergreens, with a rogue plum tree struggling for space. As with all flats, light and space were salient features. Both sitting room and first bedroom boasted two large windows, one in each case, facing the trees, giving steams of sunshine through their moving branches until midday. At lunchtime the window facing south took over, sun shining into the room which I would use as the dining room. In spite of having a new aspect, it felt familiar to me.

The elderly lady selling the flat, along with her daughter, explained the things I already knew about the area, and about the new regime of management now in operation. The usual up-grades of modern kitchen, new heating system, and double glazing to windows had been installed, and bedrooms fitted with ample, mirrored wardrobes. The flat even came with a garage and one parking place not specified.

After indicating my assurance that an offer would be put forward, subject to "searches", and architect's report, I returned to Chandlers Ford ready to proceed. It was time to turn my attention to the big "clear-out" started at Bere Close, but stalling at times. Several trips with old curtains and clothes had been made to charity shops, and now crockery and large units had to be collected by The Heart Foundation for sale in Southampton.

An unfortunate visit to Garnier Road Recycling Depot, ended in difficulties. After disposing of some electrical items, I finally threw a bag of garden waste into a skip about to be emptied. My friend would be awaiting my visit for a cup of coffee. The car was safely locked, as I took goods to various stands. Now the keys could not be found. They could only have fallen from my gloved hand into the greenery in the vast collection in the skip. Seeing my agitated state, and leaning over the fence surrounding the skips of greenery, one of the organizing men came to my side, asking what | had thrown over. Upon explanation, he looked serious and downcast, but sympathetic and said he would do what he could about the loss.

He came back with a middle-aged lady with a ready smile. She took charge of the situation, assuring me that by the end of the day, the keys would be found. Her first idea was to use a powerful magnet, saying if that did not work, the skip would be searched as it was being emptied. I was then offered a lift to Chandlers

Ford to collect my spare set of keys. On the way we were to stop in Saint Cross to explain to my friend what had happened, where I would ask my friend to drive me home, and release this kind lady from driving me farther. After a bit of persuasion, we were all seated, drinking cups of coffee. Conversation was easy, and light-hearted, mainly about Scots in general, and the oddity of some items brought to the depot for disposal, and saved by the staff for sale in the shop. We were about to leave on our different routes, when the lady's mobile rang to tell her that the keys had been found. Having expressed our thanks for the coffee and chat, I returned to the depot, much relieved, and my companion saying, it was the best day's work she had ever done.

My letter of thanks was sincere and grateful, full of praise for the kindness shown to me throughout, by all who helped in the search for my keys. Naturally, I heaped tins of biscuits on the staff as some sort of gesture, and wrote a piece, as requested, for the local newspaper, stating how professionally run I found the site. Over the following months, I would visit the site on many occasions, and receive the same degree of help and consideration, but I never met the owner again.

The sale of the house in Bere Close was given over to a local agent in Chandlers Ford, whose wife I had met quite often in the office of the church, while she was secretary to our vicar. Mr Rees had moved his business from Romsey to Winchester Road, in the business hub of Chandlers Ford, just opposite the firm where Sydney and I had arranged power of attorney for ourselves.

After viewing and assessing the property, the usual brochure was brought out, with the price displayed. During the summer, the sale had depended on an advertising board, erected in front of the house, and general knowledge that the house could be viewed. Now with the Winchester flat on the horizon, the sale of the house became a priority. Two former viewers returned, one a middle-eastern gentleman, who said he was buying it for his daughter, and had already bought a house for his nephew on the adjoining estate of Knightwood. The daughter was twelve years old, and it would have been illegal to have a property bought in her name at this age. His offer was far above the asking price, and I feared withdrawal or complications. It interested me to hear the comments of praise, and what actions would enhance the property, which had great potential for extension. The garden was universally admired, with its two levels of lawn and colourful borders. With easy access to the woodland at the side of our road, and a lane alongside the main road, it represented an appealing situation for a family.

A family from the north of England became the purchasers. They already lived in Chandlers Ford, occupying rented accommodation, where they hoped that their tenure could be extended for another few months. Twice the family came to view, and each time, I sat outside with the youngest member. He was much taken by the secret corner, with its white seat and surrounding foliage. It was hard not to hope that this family would be the ones living here.

Luck was on their side, and after a long wait, they were promised a good price for their house in the north. It did not compare well with what was normal in Chandlers Ford, but manageable. The two elder children were already friendly with a family in the cul-de-sac, and I was told later, that one spent more time in my previous home than she did in her own one. It was turning out well for everyone.

Unfortunately, at the time, I felt it best to have the legal work done by the agent's firm of solicitors, who, too late, I discovered had their office in Hertfordshire. Our old firm of Faithful and Bowker for one of whom David had caddied on Hockley golf course, was still in existence, but had been taken over by a firm with its headquarters in Portsmouth, but had a local branch in Chandlers Ford. It would have been more efficient to have used this firm to expedite completion of the sale in less than six months, which seemed unduly long.

Time and again, it seemed there was unnecessary delay. Month followed month, with the odd letter apologising for the delay, or with some document to be signed, or some fact confirmed. My surveyor had pronounced on the state of the building as being typical of those constructed in the sixties, with no immediate problems to be rectified. Each time I had expectations of exchanges taking place before Christmas. My buyers were able to extend their present lease, but too, were anxious to be in their new home by Christmas. It would be February before completion; in fact, removal took place on Saint Valentine's Day.

Neighbours and friends did not desert me during this frustrating period. There were outings and gatherings, when someone had a birthday, and I was taken to see the Saplings in Wiltshire, which had been planted in remembrance of Sydney. The family visited often, and I had not removed the small plant pots in the grass, with the flag sticks showing numbers, so that anyone inclined could have a round of putting. Most days, I went round the four holes on the lower grass and climbed the rocky steps to complete the five holes above.

I knew I would miss all this, and it made me irritable in a way I had not experienced, during any of my previous moves. I applauded the Scottish system, where sales were agreed in a few days, if there was no money impediment, and cutting out the need for the intervention of an agent.

As usual, dancing did not start for the final session of the year until September, by which time dancers were looking forward to the end of the summer break. School was back in harness. Seven new people from a rambling group were to be joining us in the newly extended hall at Saint Francis on Wednesday evenings. This proved a challenge for everyone, so that the first half hour had to be devoted to teaching steps and simple movements. Newcomers were paired with experienced dancers, who took them under their wing until formations became more familiar, and timing more accurate. By Christmas, when all had mastered some steps and several formations, the evening party was devoted to favourite dances, food and wine, brought by all. Most had a "Kit", consisting of two plates, cutlery and a wine glass [mostly plastic]. This meant that no time was wasted washing up, or clearing up. My tartan runner of fourteen feet was placed on tables running at the side of the hall, where food and wine was laid out. On one such occasion at Newbury, my "kit" went astray, but returned to me via dancing links in Andover, Salisbury, Winchester and finally, Southampton.

By early January, dancers were back in the hall, preparing for Burn's celebrations.

Dances, appropriate for such an occasion, were trawled through our dance books, and plans made for our supper, and entertainment. Previously, I had bought the haggis, neeps and tatties, and with willing hands, prepared the first course of the feast. Puddings, for which we had become famous, were usually quite simple, like Lairds Cream, a jelly dish with a good dash of whisky in its make-up.

This time, arrangements had to be different, because of my imminent move to Winchester. The pub next to the church, The Cleveland Bay, had been our last stop on many evenings, when we were served by a young neighbour during her break from university.

It was not a place that we frequented now that the young lady had met an untimely death in Spain. Her reaction to some medication during the removal of a tooth, proved fatal. The community felt this tragic loss very keenly, and no one felt at ease ending the evening there, until memories had faded somewhat.

The Cleveland Bay, would provide haggis and vegetables, and allow music to be played while the haggis was brought in by one of the kitchen staff. We were allocated an area at the far end, with a window at its end. Suddenly, I realized that all I had to do this time was collect money from our eighteen diners, and pay the bill. Most of us had a form of "Lairds Cream" and those who declined were not charged. Drinks were paid for individually.

The staff entered into the spirit of the evening, standing round for The Address to The Haggis, and laughing at the address to "The lassies", and its response. A disclaimer was read out stating that this performance bore no resemblance to an official "Burns" celebration. We left, thanking the staff for their service and indulgence, and inviting fellow customers to join us in Saint Francis hall for dancing. This was not followed up, I am disappointed to say.

As so often happens, when unexpected, everything came together. All searches had been carried out, copies of leases read and approved. I was safe to dispose of my large furniture to The Heart Foundation. The elegant walnut and glass unit was taken away, being one inch over the desired width, and fetched the charity a good price. EMEAS, in Winchester took three beds, but for obvious reasons would not be able to sell the mattresses. The single mattresses were easy to bring downstairs, for take away by the council. The doubles posed a problem getting round the curve on the staircase. By taking a painting from the wall, I was able to turn them round the curve and let them take their own course over the rest of the steps. Getting them to the door of the garage, seemed relatively straightforward. Hearing of other peoples' experiences, our loft was relatively under used. A grandson soon pulled forth the folding ladder and brought down the old television, and several chairs, kept there for the dancers' end of season dance in our garden.

B.0.A.S. was a charity I had heard of, situated just north of Winchester, helping young people with "Special needs" to have an active life tending a garden, looking after poultry and animal husbandry. Their produce was of the highest quality, and sold well giving a sense of achievement to all participants. This was the ideal place for my gardening equipment to be offered. A person from the charity arrived in a large estate car, and loaded up his boot with my lawn mower, fork, loppers, and a basin full of smaller items, useful in growing vegetables and pruning bushes.

It was time to think of a removal firm, and a friend recommended Bradbeers, a firm in Romsey, which had moved some furniture for him. This was the choice, until someone asked why I was not engaging a more local company based in Chandlers Ford. The prospect of having this company looked good, and I decided to ask for a quotation. A young man arrived to assess the task, and upon hearing my Scottish accent, informed me that his family came from Dunblane, and that his brother had been at school there with Andy Murray. The town and its surroundings were well known to me, having holidayed at "The Hydro" on a few occasions. The deal was sealed, and the whole undertaking proved enjoyable and fun. David and June arrived to lend a hand. The day dawned sunny and warm for February.

For some reason, one of the removal men had care of his daughter that morning, and "asked a huge favour", if could she come with him, on the assurance that she would sit and read her books in the cab of his van. She was brought in and became a valued member of the team, running upstairs for items, and serving pancakes with the many cups of tea consumed during the morning.

By one o'clock, it was time to lock up for the last time, which I did on my own. David and June had gone ahead to receive entry to the flat, while I left the keys with my agent. When I parked at The Normans, I was shocked to find the removal van closed up and David standing on the doorstep. The owner's daughter was refusing to hand over the keys, saying her mother was in hospital. This was the case when I visited the agent selling the property, who had agreed the hand-over to be at twelve noon that day. He was instrumental in having the keys collected from the hospital, or somewhere, and made immediately available to me. My heart was pounding during the uncertain delay. Our plans for a meal at The Queen's Head with the removal men, had been thrown up in the air by this manoeuvre.

The little girl had been collected by her mother. The three men had bought sandwiches, and were eating them in the cab of the van. It was well after one o'clock, and by the time I returned with the keys, it was to find that a spare set had been handed over by the owner's relative and entry had been gained. I was met in the forecourt, as I parked the car by the youngest member of the team with a wave towards the building and the cry "we're in".

The usual turmoil of a removal hit me at the front door of the flat, as I stepped over boxes and cases in the tiny hallway. In the kitchen, I found June on hands and knees, having scrubbed the kitchen floor, and now sorting out the contents of cupboards, into containers of 'best by' dates. The out of date items far outweighed the number of useable foodstuffs, like sugar and salt. Most went into a bag to be taken by David to the refuse bins at the back of the building. I felt quite smug, thinking of my efforts at Bere Close, to present the new owners with a home, cleaned and polished, and a small box of books and toys left for their youngest member to take to his favourite hide-out in the corner of the garden. By mid-afternoon, the work was complete. Only the arrangements of smaller items of furniture, was still to be decided. The removal men left, with a large tip to cover the aborted lunch, assuring me that if any piece of furniture required to be moved in the flat, one of them would attend to it.

I was able to recommend this firm to a dancing couple, moving from Southampton to Plymouth. Later when I did seek their help, they were able to describe the property in Plymouth, and its large garden, most of which would be turned into a vegetable plot, with some bee hives.

David and June had to leave before mealtime, but would send my granddaughter the following day as reinforcement, to hang curtains and generally lend a hand. The sun shone, as it had done since first light, and the air was warm for mid-February. In spite of the lunchtime set back, it had been a most enjoyable and unique Valentine's Day. Always thoughtful and considerate, David and June made me promise to have my evening meal at

The Queens Head, knowing that that would be my first step outside my new home and best done into company.

A fire blazed in the hearth of the pub, and a jolly sound filled the air. I was shown to a table by the window, and soon had a plate of lamb chops and vegetables placed in front of me, I then realized how hungry I was, having survived on cups of tea, and the odd pancake. The couple at the table next to mine, swiped all of their cutlery to the floor accidentally, and their apology led to conversation. They lived at Stanmore, an estate of which I knew almost nothing, since it did not exist in my previous life in Winchester.

My television was not operational, but I still had my portable radio for news items. I was dependent on my mobile telephone for calls for a few days, until B.T. had me online.

David called to alert me that Elaine, was on her way by train, so at the appropriate time I left home to walk back from the station with her. It was another dry and sunny day, as I walked along Southgate Street, remembering Doctor Gibson's surgery and Saint Thomas church. A feeling of slight irritation surfaced, where a building had changed from its former use.

With Elaine's help, curtains soon hung from curtain rails left by the previous owner, paintings and mirrors hung from hooks on the walls, and the flat took on a lived touch. I gloried in the evergreen trees facing me from the settee in the sitting room, their branches swaying in the breeze and the odd bird hopping up or down. Sunshine flooded the room through the bare branches. Our day was not to be one entirely of toil, and around one o'clock, Elaine and I crossed to The Queens Head for a substantial lunch, she choosing a vegetarian dish, and I a piece of fish. Later, we walked along the path, through the water meadows to Saint Cross, and back along the quaint road of Back Street, and into Saint Faiths Road, lined with Edwardian houses, reminiscent of Duthie Terrace in Aberdeen. The village Hall and walled allotments were there, as they had been for years, and the school with its sports ground on the opposite side of the road. Our eyes sought the hillside of Saint Catherine's hill, but decided that would be for another time. Elaine left to be home early in the evening, while I appraised the work done that day.

A visit to the pub was repeated by me next day, when I was seated at the same table near the window, and treated as a regular customer by the waitress, who asked about 'my daughter' and remembered her ordering a vegetarian dish. The experience added to my confidence of the area, and although I did not return for a meal for some time, it remained my first choice.

It was time to consider any improvements I wished to make to the flat. The hallway was very dark, so along with new white doors to each room, it required a glass door to the kitchen, to give better light to the entrance where a tall bookcase had been placed. A neighbour from Channdlers Ford, who was a surveyor, took charge of the work, even taking me to the store where I could make my choices. The outcome was a great success, although, it took me some time to get used to visitors having a view into the kitchen as they entered.

I countered this by hanging a painting of that old bridge at Invercauld on the wall opposite the door, and placing a huge glass container with a plant inside on the kitchen surround.

Only the bathroom had to be discarded. The water filling the cast iron bath was luke warm by the time ablutions were complete, so a modern bath, made from some less chilling material was installed with the rest of the suite. Now, for me, the interesting part began, that of choosing colour schemes and ordering fabrics to replace the curtains hung by Elaine and me, as a temporary measure. Southampton stores offered a wide range of materials, but it was in Winchester that I found The Rennie Macintosh design that I wanted. It had a mauve and green design, and stood out amongst other materials on display. I ordered metres, with a good allowance for matching up of the design. My friend hanging the new doors, remarked that my job seemed more complicated than his, when he saw me down on hands and knees on the sitting room floor, measuring, cutting and matching. When hung on either side of the two windows, the result brought much admiration of the design, I had chosen.

Dancing was not interrupted by Sydney's illness. It was the habit of clubs to break from the end of June till the beginning part of September, when nights were cooler. Several dancers had gone from the area, and our numbers were sadly depleted, until an old stalwart returned, bringing three new recruits, and we were able to continue with the fee of one pound fifty each evening. Crisis arose when the education authority decided to change the status of the church / school hall, and that a charge of nineteen pounds an hour would be levied. This was far above the amount we were prepared to pay; almost six pounds each for the evening. A meeting was held in the church, and the decision taken that we hired the hall in the Methodist church in Chandlers Ford, for half that amount, although it would be smaller and carpeted. This was certainly more convenient for me, and for some others, where public transport could be used. For nine months dancing took place there, but dancers became irritated by the carpeted floor, and poor facilities, so somewhere else would have to be found with a wooden floor.

Saint Faiths village Hall in Saint Cross was free on Wednesday evenings. Covnenient for me, but not for everyone. That is where we are for the present, with good facilities, and a wooden floor.

Fourteen

Sydney's niece, Norma, and her husband were now living in Canada and had visited us in Chandlers Ford a few weeks before Sydney's final spell in hospital. It had been their usual spirited and teasing encounter, with fond requests that Canada be the next holiday destination and not Aberdeen; after all, what was the difference: you paid a lot of money, sat for a long time and were met by car at the other end!

Since they had seen Sydney so recently, I thought it unnecessary for them to make the journey again for the funeral service. A period of uncertainty lasted for a week, before I had to agree that I should go to Canada, where a suitable memorial would be placed somewhere on their hundred acre property, to remember their uncle. After so many refusals of hospitality by him over the years, it seemed ironic and quite comical that his ashes would be spread on the outskirts of Ottawa.

My cousin, Elma, was invited to accompany me to Canada. The following year, we boarded a flight to Ottawa, to be met by Norma and Davie at the airport. At the airport before leaving Britain, we found ourselves in conversation with a man from Huntly, who had known my late brother-in law, Theodore

[Teddy]. Everyone in Huntly and around knew Teddy, and knew the secret greeting exchanged between him and the local minister; hands raised and then lowered with three claps, maybe something from schooldays.

The traditional house in Kanata adjoined a garage area, over which a suite of comfortable rooms had been added. Elma and I had our own little flat there overlooking "The fairy garden". Here, the granddaughter of the house had planted flowers with bells, and hung fairies from branches of trees and strung fairy lights along the pathway. Her brother, although just ten years old drove the tractor and golf buggy competently. A nine hole golf course was being established towards a row of trees lining the roadway towards Kanata. It offered climbs up slopes and various hazards, including a burn, half hidden in its wild surrounds. A wooden seat, placed at the top of the bank just before the trees, held a plaque in memory of Sydney where his ashes would be scattered. It was the ideal location, and peace descended upon us at that time.

This was Norma and Davie's retirement home, but almost by accident, a new business was to emerge. During the winter, when Lake Constance, which abutted their mini-estate, froze over, bears were finding their way through the fence surrounding the house. Suitable, strong fencing had to be purchased, and after protecting his own property, friends asked him to order a supply for them.

The first essential was somewhere to store the fencing until friends could collect their supply. A Nissan hut was bought for storage, and demand became so large, that imports from Europe, through the U.S. became normal trade. "Deer Fencing Canada" was established. A colleague, also retired, deputised when required and it was he who took Elma and me for a day in Gatineau Park, where we had views of the Saint Lawrence river far below. There were bogs with beavers constructing their lodges, and a myriad of birds and insects. It would have been so easy to lose one's way on the intersecting trails, with signs of places we had never heard of. I was determined to see the lake which bore my name, and set off to the edge of the wood which marked the boundary. It was very rough-going, with no discerning path, and when reached was difficult to get near to its edge. Seaplanes were taking tourists over the lake at its far end, landing and taking off from the water. I had seen my lake, and now had to find a route back. I chose a route away from the wood, but this was taking me away from my destination, and I would soon be lost. The sound of Alfie, the Old English Sheep Dog of the house barking at me from my outward route, persuaded me that I had no alternative but to cross the rough ground with its holes and clods of earth.

I returned a very muddied specimen, having fallen several times without hurt.

Elma and I wished to visit Niagara Falls, planning to stay there for a few days. Our travel would be by Greyhound coach from Kanata. Having visited the well documented attractions of "The Falls City" and crossed to the American side with excellent views of "The Falls", we asked the staff of the hotel where we were staying, where we could eat away from the tourist mass. They directed us to 'The Frying Saucer' just beyond the central area. There we discovered a more local menu, and met with an eclectic number of diners, with an appetite for all things Scottish. Elma was able to relate the climbing achievements of her brother, and her son, and describe her own up-bringing in the Outer Hebrides. The first words her mother learned to say in Gaelic was 'Is the bull in the field today?". He was large and fierce, and nowhere was fenced.

A problem arose for us with Greyhound Coaches. The day we had planned to leave, the timetable had changed, and our arrival in Ottawa, where we were to be picked up by Davie, was uncertain. We both had mobile telephones with us, but found it impossible to get in touch with our hosts. A kind man at Reception would help by sending a message to his office in Ottawa who might be able to contact our host, whose home was thirty miles from the coach station.

It was lunch time, and once again we were guided to "a diner", near the coach station. Immediately we entered, Elma and I sensed that we were an intrusion. Several brawny men sat at tables, making loud conversation.

They stared at us, and all went silent. A girl behind a curtain, appeared and went back to fetch her menu list which she handed to Elma with a smirk. Not deterred, we chose our lunch. The hub bub of conversation arose again, with many looks in our direction, but we ploughed through huge plates of "Diners' Special", and paid at the desk. As we left, Elma could not resist turning to the bare-armed men and saying in an American accent "Have a good day, lads". There was time to wander along a nearby street, serving the needs of local residents, and with a good jeweller where we were able to buy a gift for our hosts, and reminders of our visit to Niagara. Two hours later than expected, we boarded a Greyhound coach for Toronto and Ottawa. To our relief, Davie was at the coach station to meet us for the journey back to Kanata.

Their son Michael, lived a short distance from Kanata, just by the mighty river Ottawa, where we were taken by the grandchildren to explore its shore and marvel at its volume of water. At Christmas, I received a brooch of small shells collected from the river and painted by a "fairy".

Our final treat was to be taken on a cruise round the islands in the Saint Lawrence river, where the rich of previous generations had built their family retreats. With binoculars, we could view the mansions amidst the greenery of their gardens, and the landing stages for big or small yachts.

It was indeed a very different land we had visited, and were now leaving. The airplane about to be boarded, would take us over the North Pole and back to London, and Hampshire.

My mind did not turn to further travel, until, by accident, I received a brochure from a firm with whom dancers had travelled to Scotland, Europe, and Cyprus. Dawn and Richard were good friends now and had attended our golden wedding celebrations in Winchester Guildhall some years before. The destination was Peru. The Incas of Peru had occupied my father's mind during my teenage years, and his interest and studies had caught my interest very much then. What an opportunity! The deadline for booking was one week hence, but in spite of the enormous cost, it only took me a second to sign up for this adventure.

Most of the tour passengers flew out of Madrid to Lima, and I was amongst them.

Although occupying a seat far from the others, after food, I was able to sleep for nearly all of the flight.

Lima was drenched, as usual, in its veil of coastal fog /drizzle /Scotch mist, but our stay would only be for two nights and the hotel was sumptuous. It seemed our progress to higher levels was to be taken in stages; the first a flight to Arequipa, a city to the south of Lima. The huge man-made hill in the centre of Lima intrigued all of us.

The flight to Arequipa was magical. Straining from the window, I could see villages more than two thousand feet down in a valley, while almost touching the sides of the mountains through which the plane was flying. I saw the volcano, Amputo, up which a young girl had been escorted for her death as a sacrifice to the Sun God. I was to learn more about Junita and her tragic walk up the mountain in the museum.

Up at five o clock for the journey by coach and train to Machu Picchu. The vegetation was changing, the fields were smaller as we entered the upper jungle. Alpaca grazed near run-down cottages of stone. Before us towered high mountains, their tops white with snow. Our climb to Machu Picchu was gentle until the city was reached and we alighted from the train, far below the ancient relics. A fleet of coaches awaited tourists to take them over hairpin bends to the monuments. All was well until two coaches met at a hairpin bend. Drivers were reluctant to go forward or reverse at such a point. No vehicle rolled down the thousand feet drop to the valley below.

There are no words to describe the wonder of Machu Picchu, with its ancient terraces and stone buildings. It will always deserve a personal visit.

Lake Titicaca is quite vast, with the island Uros, far out from shore, which is formed entirely of reeds. From the island, we sailed to an area where craft items were made for sale to passengers. At the far end, we disembarked to visit a small village with a communal vegetable garden. We had brought books and crayons, and small gifts for the children as requested by our tour guide, but unfortunately it was holiday time for the children. I was able to sit with an old grandma, who received my gifts with a hug.

A steam ship, The Yavari, built in Liverpool and brought to Puno o n the shores of Lake Titicaca, in eighteen sixty was on view. This ship had been transported, piece by piece across The Andes, a distance of three thousand miles, and took six years to arrive.

In Cusco, Aramas Square was an interesting place to relax, with balconies overlooking its foliage, and music being played by the tables where coffee and meals were being served.

Our guide of two days earlier joined me, and our conversation revealed that she had met my granddaughter, Elaine, when she was in Cusco for several weeks the previous summer, caring for deprived children. She approved of the hints given to me by Elaine for my protection; police numbers, and which taxis were reliable.

The magnificent Cathedral stood at one corner of the square, beckoning me to visit its interior stone work and solid silver altar. Treasures abounded and each time I visited the square, I was drawn inside.

Richard, our tour operator, had arranged a meal for us at a local restaurant, serving ethnic Peruvian food. It would be reached on foot, and on the way there was much speculation as to what we would be served. Guinea pig, llama and wild pig was served to us on wooden plates, washed down with cocao, that drink aimed at reducing altitude sickness, from which, happily I never suffered. I did not care much for this drink anyway. Llamas and guinea pigs were to be seen everywhere, especially around Lake Titicaca. Birds of prey were perched on the buildings; some species of vulture, I believe.

My last action after visiting The Sacred Valley, was to throw a piece of broken branch into the great river, Urubamba, which ran by the hotel we were staying in, in the hope that it would reach the Amazon, and be carried out into the Atlantic Ocean.

Again, our flight to Lima took us over and between high peaks. I had felt at home with these people. My height of just touching five feet, felt normal in this country, where even the men were not much taller than me. I had enjoyed their hospitality, their music and treasures beyond imagination.

Next summer, I made my stay in Aberdeen and Braemar, where I met up with Elma, and her group of ramblers. Together, we visited The Queens Drive and climbed part of the path leading to the top of The Cow Hill to enjoy the view. We looked over the gate into the garden of Roy Cottage, where I had been born, and walked past our grandmother's cottage in Castleton Terrace. While Elma, bagged "Munroes" with her party, I visited Craig Choinnich and An Car Prop, which brought back memories of walks with my father. Huge ant heaps had formed in the wood surrounding Mart Lodge Estate, and I was able to climb over the fence to marvel at the industry of these insects.

Unfortunately, a leap over a burn did not end well. The far bank was slippery and I fell back onto a pointed boulder. Water rushed over me, soaking all of my clothes. Upon attempting to rise, a sharp pain struck the base of my spine. There was no one abroad on the hillside to help me, but inch by inch, I edged closer to a sapling growing out of the bank and was able to pull myself from the burn. There was no alternative but to gain the path, and no matter how painful, make it to Chapel Brae. I must have presented a strange sight to the woman exercising her dog, who was my first contact. My black suit still dripped water, in spite of a stiff breeze coming from the west. The black suit fitted all occasions, and travelling light, was my only garb. Setting out early in a morning required a jacket to begin with, and later its sleeves could be tied round my waist when the temperature rose. The lady with the black Labrador did help me along where the path allowed, advising me all the time to visit a doctor in the village. She left me at her front door on Chapel Brae. Almost dry now, I was glad to reach the cafe' at the foot, which was once owned by Jack Sloan, my young sister's champion and had sold all manner of Highland goods.

The Invercauld Hotel offered me a cheerful return and the assurance that my black suit would be pressed within half an hour. My ground floor room, with its small conservatory and comfortable armchairs, was a welcome sanctuary.

I was invited by a fellow guest in the hotel to accompany her to the chapel at Mar Lodge. Although I was familiar with Mar Lodge, itself, I had never entered the chapel, commissioned by The Duchess of Fife, daughter of the queen. It was typical of its era, a real gem, intimate and now serving a wide range of worshipers.

One more day remained for wandering in the village, where I had tea with a former pupil of my class at Braemar School. She reminded me of our then new headmaster, and our removal to Castleton Hall, with its polished wooden floors, while the school was being refurbished.

Next day, I bid farewell to Elma and the ramblers, thanked the hotel staff for their help, and gingerly boarded the bus for Aberdeen. My niece was able to confirm that my back injury had caused a black and blue mark six inches in diameter at the base of my back. Still I did not seek medical advice, but sheltered under firm, elasticated underwear.

Fifteen

SYDNEY AND I HAD TRAVELLED EXTENSIVELY IN THE WEST OF Scotland during his working life with the Forestry Commission, but always by car. Loch Lubnaig was one of our favourite stopping places, where cabins were let to holiday-makers, by The Commission. Although near to Arrochar, it felt remote, and was popular, bringing in lucrative rents to the government.

Much talk had gone on about the West Highland railway, which we had viewed from roadways at various points. I now decided that I should use this form of transport, and pass judgement on the opinions that it was not to be missed. A tour was to leave Edinburgh, which included a tour by bus to where the railway could be boarded. I took a flight to Edinburgh and joined the company of other tourists waiting to board the train for a normal journey by rail to our hotel in Newtonmore. From the railway line t he views were more spectacular than I expected, so much so, that some foreign students were standing on their seats to appreciate the receding scenery. The hotel was welcoming, and next day we were driven by coach to the station where the steam train could be boarded for Mallaig.

The remoteness and beauty of the route excited the passengers, most of whom, unlike me, had never experienced a journey by steam. My interest lay in The Commission's pulp mill at Corpach, which the railway passed by. I had visited the pulp mill once before and marvelled at the amount of timber it could devour. Tons of British timber was devoured each day along with supplies from farther afield; Finland and Norway, to be turned into cardboard and other day to day materials.

On our return from Mallaig, the train again crossed the spectacular, curved viaduct, but this time stopped so that passengers could admire the statue in remembrance of the commandoes who trained in this area for war with Germany; fearless young men who travelled the hills and flew their planes through narrow glens to win victory for us. For all of us, standing before the memorial, it was a moment of gratitude and reflection.

I did not continue the tour with the rest of the tourists, instead hopped off at Newtonmore station where I was able to board a train from Glasgow, going to Inverness. It is a single line, subject to the timing of trains using the line in opposite directions. On the platform, there is a telephone where a prospective passenger can call for information, but that proved unhelpful for the two people hoping to board a train for Glasgow. There were seats for about twenty people. The sun shone and the scenery was lovely. Two people moved away, muttering something about delays. A man from the Isle of Skye sat next to me, admiring the hills, all of which he had climbed. I took the opportunity to ask had he met a girl called Sadie, from Edinburgh, who Sydney and I used to take to dances, and who had left to live on Skye many years ago along with a doctor and his wife who now had a thriving sheep farm on the island. This man was able to confirm that Sadie was happy and had made many friends. We parted, he first for Glasgow, and me some time later for Inverness and Aberdeen, where I would stay in The Royal Hotel with my relatives, as was my custom.

Aberdeen Train Station was bustling, as usual, still with people working at the harbour, and obviously in the oil business. Having seen my family, I failed to hire a car the following day for my journey up Deeside, so my plans had to change. Before leaving for the Highland railway, I had done a dummy run on the computer, so that I would have all the documents and information required by the companies hiring vehicles. All went well until I hit the buffer of "age". The garage I approached had an age limit of eighty years for insurance. Some companies set the barrier at seventy five. Only Enterprise, I found out later, extended this to eighty five years; such an unfair blow, since I could have driven my own car the six hundred miles to Aberdeen, and then carried on to any destination.

Over the space of three days, I was able to follow much of the trail I had set myself.

The old Deeside Road, before the turnpike, which ran past our cottage of Fairview, fascinated me and I planned to follow its route as far as possible. My starting point was north of Union Street at what I believed was the start of The Hardgate. This I followed, then past The Royal Hotel, up Windmill Brae, across Crown Street into Langstane Place, and onward parallel to Holburn Street, to the Bridge Of Dee. The made-up road veering west, followed the route, passing Fairview and Loirsbank Farm where the fields flooded each year, and for which the government had paid compensation. Now it was the site for up market housing. The old landmark of The Shakkin' Brig was hardly to be seen, its peeling white paint and sagging timbers hidden in bushes and saplings. The Bramble Roadie, part of this ancient track, was bounded on each side by a boulder dyke, hidden in places by brambles and thistles. Perhaps, it will be kept as a feature of the new development. Houses on the northern side of the path were "new" although several years old now, and did not intrude. Their sitting rooms were on the first floor, giving extensive views of the river and Ardoe House, peeking out from behind surrounding trees. The houses built on the flooding fields would not inhibit their view.

The path rose towards the Allan Park, and two paths presented themselves as possibly authentic. I followed the one through the park, between banks of rhododendrons, not knowing where it branched to higher ground. It passed near to Culblean Cottage, my childhood home, and I gained its route, passing McDonald's Farm down in the hollow, and going through a garden in Bieldside, which my father used, and pointed out as an old right of way. I was then on the main road which was part of the old turnpike. The path branched off again to go behind some houses and along the edge of the golf course, into a little wood lined with boulders, but only on one side. To end this part of my day's journey, I crossed over the made-up road leading to Rudolf Steiner's homes for handicapped children, and the ferry, crossing the Dee, to Blairs College, a Catholic seminary for students preparing for the priesthood. I was now in Murtle.

The following day, I caught a bus to Culter, alighting at the stop for the school where I had once been a pupil, and walked along the little-changed main road to where a road led down the side of Culter Burn to the paper mill, the main employer in this small town. There, I was able to cross the burn by holding on to a rickety wooden rail, and find a path between some buildings, going upwards to behind that popular stopping place for vans and lorries, known as "Pie Jean's". It called to mind the "diners" in Canada. I had once eaten my lunch there, when a storm struck Culter, and it was impossible to return home for lunch.

A stiff breeze had sprung up and I decided to board a bus for Banchory, and view parts of the old road from the top deck, as it passed by farm buildings and disappeared into woods near Drumoak.

Arriving in Banchory, the first place to be visited had to be the river Feugh, irrespective of any connection with the old road. It was, as it always is; water crashing over great stones into narrow slits, a noise like thunder as it made its way under the roadway to join the river Dee. Some of the magic and wildness of the falls, was now inhibited by a "safety bridge" and fencing, so that no one could now experience the thrill of getting close to the deluge and feeling the spray rise from the boulders, as water crashed over them.

The old route was to be followed, and I quickly left the Feugh for the end of the golf course. Here the path followed the river, several feet beneath a steep bank. A heron was standing sentinel on a little island on the far side. I watched him until he flew off with some sort of a catch. The route was well used, but disappeared into brambles and thistles. A path led over the golf course to the main road, where I found a Cafe' to eat and relax before boarding a bus taking me back to Aberdeen.

The last part of my search for the old road was by taking the bus to Aboyne, some miles on from Banchory. Again, I crossed the Dee by a solid, modern road bridge, ignoring the temptation to visit the small village of Birse, and veering west towards Glen Tanar. I was reminded of my painting of this part of the river by the Marquis of Huntly which had been in all the homes we had occupied. There was a path of sorts by the river along which I walked for some distance, but did not find the exact location. After sitting in the sun on a wall skirting the made-up road, I was driven back by the storm of hail which had threatened before the sun came out. Weather can be very fickle in this area. After a bit of a soaking and windswept, I took refuge in The Boat Inn for refreshment before returning to Aberdeen and the far south of England. The search had been successful in places, and thoroughly enjoyable. Perhaps someone in the future will carry out a more comprehensive venture.

REturning to Winchester, the Polish family, who had occupied one of the flats at 'The Normans' and with whom I had become friendly, returned to Poland just before Christmas. The two school boys had settled well here, but their new baby brother would not spend his early years in Winchester. We parted emotionally, exchanging small gifts.I meant every word of my promise to visit Poland one day, and this came sooner than expected. Elma, in Turnberry, knowing of my promise, forwarded an offer she had seen in a newspaper of a few days in Krakow, with a note to say she would accompany me. Our first idea was to travel together from Stanstead, but neither of us was keen to fly from that airport. In the end, she was able to fly from Edinburgh and I from Gatwick, with only half an hour between arrival times.

We were both entranced by the Polish city. Our hotel was just yards away from the main square. The streets were clean and the bakeries packed with newly-made treats. It had the feeling of enclosure, typical of most mid-European cities. The boys were at school, thirty kilometres from Krakow, but their mother, Patricia visited me for a day, taking me for tea at an exclusive restaurant overlooking The Square. Saint Mary's Cathedral stood in one corner, with its trumpeter appearing on his little balcony to blow his trumpet each hour. As usual, Elma and I went our separate ways. I did not want to visit the death camp with its gruesome relics. Memories of terrible atrocities carried out there was something I carried with me from childhood, and did not want to be reminded of. I did visit The Schindler Factory, and the ghetto, remembering Doctor Gebhart, my one-time colleague.

After much walking along the Vistula river and viewing of The Castle, a rest was needed before dinner at a nearby restaurant, and a concert recommended by the hotel staff.

I flew back to Edinburgh with Elma, by Easy Jet. Had she been returning with the same company that brought her, she would have been seriously delayed because of a strike. People found it quite comical that I had reached Edinburgh via Krakow. Weather was colder in Edinburgh and the streets dirtier.

A sense of gladness came over me as I boarded a 'sleeper' bound for London and Winchester. For the first time of my travelling up and down the country, I felt I was going home to the south. It was not just the place where I lived , but "home". Previously, any journey to the north had been "going home", now that was reversed. My affection for Aberdeenshire has not waned, but my clan's war cry of "Tulach Ard" to [The high hillock] now just means the top of Saint Catherine's Hill.